The Future of Home Health Care

WORKSHOP SUMMARY

Victoria Weisfeld and Tracy A. Lustig, *Rapporteurs*

Forum on Aging, Disability, and Independence

Board on Health Sciences Policy

Division of Behavioral and Social Sciences and Education

INSTITUTE OF MEDICINE *AND*
NATIONAL RESEARCH COUNCIL
OF THE NATIONAL ACADEMIES

THE NATIONAL ACADEMIES PRESS
Washington, D.C.
www.nap.edu

THE NATIONAL ACADEMIES PRESS   500 Fifth Street, NW   Washington, DC 20001

NOTICE: The workshop that is the subject of this workshop summary was approved by the Governing Board of the National Research Council, whose members are drawn from the councils of the National Academy of Sciences, the National Academy of Engineering, and the Institute of Medicine.

This activity was supported by contracts between the National Academy of Sciences and the Alliance for Home Health Quality and Innovation, the American Academy of Home Care Medicine, the American Nurses Association, the American Physical Therapy Association, Axxess, the Community Health Accreditation Program, Home Instead Senior Care, the National Alliance for Caregiving, and Unity Point at Home. The views presented in this publication do not necessarily reflect the views of the organizations or agencies that provided support for the activity.

International Standard Book Number-13:   978-0-309-36753-0
International Standard Book Number-10:   0-309-36753-0

Additional copies of this workshop summary are available for sale from the National Academies Press, 500 Fifth Street, NW, Keck 360, Washington, DC 20001; (800) 624-6242 or (202) 334-3313; http://www.nap.edu.

For more information about the Institute of Medicine, visit the IOM home page at: **www.iom.edu.**

The serpent has been a symbol of long life, healing, and knowledge among almost all cultures and religions since the beginning of recorded history. The serpent adopted as a logotype by the Institute of Medicine is a relief carving from ancient Greece, now held by the Staatliche Museen in Berlin.

Suggested citation: IOM (Institute of Medicine) and NRC (National Research Council). 2015. *The future of home health care: Workshop summary.* Washington, DC: The National Academies Press.

THE NATIONAL ACADEMIES
Advisers to the Nation on Science, Engineering, and Medicine

The **National Academy of Sciences** is a private, nonprofit, self-perpetuating society of distinguished scholars engaged in scientific and engineering research, dedicated to the furtherance of science and technology and to their use for the general welfare. Upon the authority of the charter granted to it by the Congress in 1863, the Academy has a mandate that requires it to advise the federal government on scientific and technical matters. Dr. Ralph J. Cicerone is president of the National Academy of Sciences.

The **National Academy of Engineering** was established in 1964, under the charter of the National Academy of Sciences, as a parallel organization of outstanding engineers. It is autonomous in its administration and in the selection of its members, sharing with the National Academy of Sciences the responsibility for advising the federal government. The National Academy of Engineering also sponsors engineering programs aimed at meeting national needs, encourages education and research, and recognizes the superior achievements of engineers. Dr. C. D. Mote, Jr., is president of the National Academy of Engineering.

The **Institute of Medicine** was established in 1970 by the National Academy of Sciences to secure the services of eminent members of appropriate professions in the examination of policy matters pertaining to the health of the public. The Institute acts under the responsibility given to the National Academy of Sciences by its congressional charter to be an adviser to the federal government and, upon its own initiative, to identify issues of medical care, research, and education. Dr. Victor J. Dzau is president of the Institute of Medicine.

The **National Research Council** was organized by the National Academy of Sciences in 1916 to associate the broad community of science and technology with the Academy's purposes of furthering knowledge and advising the federal government. Functioning in accordance with general policies determined by the Academy, the Council has become the principal operating agency of both the National Academy of Sciences and the National Academy of Engineering in providing services to the government, the public, and the scientific and engineering communities. The Council is administered jointly by both Academies and the Institute of Medicine. Dr. Ralph J. Cicerone and Dr. C. D. Mote, Jr., are chair and vice chair, respectively, of the National Research Council.

www.national-academies.org

PLANNING COMMITTEE FOR A WORKSHOP ON THE FUTURE OF HOME HEALTH CARE[1]

BRUCE LEFF (*Co-Chair*), Professor of Medicine, Johns Hopkins University School of Medicine

ELIZABETH MADIGAN (*Co-Chair*), Associate Professor of Nursing, Frances Payne Bolton School of Nursing, Case Western Reserve University

CHRISTINE E. BISHOP, Atran Professor of Labor Economics and Director of the Ph.D. Program at the Heller School of Social Policy and Management, Brandeis University

BARBARA B. CITARELLA, Founder, RBC Limited

THOMAS E. EDES, Executive Director, Geriatrics and Extended Care, U.S. Department of Veterans Affairs

MARGHERITA C. LABSON, Executive Director, Home Care Program, The Joint Commission

TERESA L. LEE, Executive Director, Alliance for Home Health Quality and Innovation

ANNE MONTGOMERY, Senior Policy Analyst, Altarum Institute

IOM Staff

TRACY A. LUSTIG, Forum Director
Y. CRYSTI PARK, Senior Program Assistant
ANDREW M. POPE, Director, Board on Health Sciences Policy

---

[1] Institute of Medicine and National Research Council planning committees are solely responsible for organizing the workshop, identifying topics, and choosing speakers. The responsibility for the published workshop summary rests with the workshop rapporteurs and the institution.

IOM-NRC FORUM ON AGING, DISABILITY, AND INDEPENDENCE[1]

ALAN M. JETTE (*Co-Chair*), Boston University School of Public Health, Boston, MA

JOHN W. ROWE (*Co-Chair*), Columbia University, New York, NY

KELLY BUCKLAND, National Council on Independent Living, Washington, DC

JOE CALDWELL, National Council on Aging, Washington, DC

MARGARET L. CAMPBELL, National Institute on Disability and Rehabilitation Research, Washington, DC

EILEEN M. CRIMMINS, University of Southern California, Los Angeles

PEGGYE DILWORTH-ANDERSON, Gillings School of Global Public Health, University of North Carolina at Chapel Hill

STEVEN C. EDELSTEIN, PHI, Bronx, NY

THOMAS E. EDES, U.S. Department of Veterans Affairs, Washington, DC

TERRY FULMER, Bouvé College of Health Sciences, Northeastern University, Boston, MA

NAOMI L. GERBER, Center for the Study of Chronic Illness and Disability, George Mason University, Fairfax, VA

ROBERT HORNYAK, Administration for Community Living, Washington, DC

LISA I. IEZZONI, Harvard Medical School, Boston, MA

JUDITH D. KASPER, Johns Hopkins Bloomberg School of Public Health, Baltimore, MD

KATHY KREPCIO, John J. Heldrich Center for Workforce Development, Rutgers, The State University of New Jersey, New Brunswick, NJ

NANCY LUNDEBJERG, American Geriatrics Society, New York, NY

RHONDA MEDOWS, United HealthCare, Washington, DC

LARRY MINNIX, LeadingAge, Washington, DC

ARI NE'EMAN, National Council on Disability, Washington, DC

RENÉ SEIDEL, The SCAN Foundation, Long Beach, CA

JACK W. SMITH, U.S. Department of Defense, Falls Church, VA

RICHARD SUZMAN, National Institute on Aging, Bethesda, MD

---

[1] Institute of Medicine and National Research Council forums do not issue, review, or approve individual documents. The responsibility for the published summary rests with the workshop rapporteurs and the institution.

Reviewers

This workshop summary has been reviewed in draft form by individuals chosen for their diverse perspectives and technical expertise, in accordance with procedures approved by the National Research Council's Report Review Committee. The purpose of this independent review is to provide candid and critical comments that will assist the institution in making its published workshop summary as sound as possible and to ensure that the workshop summary meets institutional standards for objectivity, evidence, and responsiveness to the study charge. The review comments and draft manuscript remain confidential to protect the integrity of the process. We wish to thank the following individuals for their review of this workshop summary:

AMY BERMAN, The John A. Hartford Foundation
MARGARET CAMPBELL, National Institute on Disability and Rehabilitation Research
REBECCA CONANT, University of California, San Francisco, School of Medicine
LINDA DeCHERRIE, Mount Sinai Hospital
WARREN HEBERT, HomeCare Association of Louisiana
MELISSA O'CONNOR, Villanova University

Although the reviewers listed above have provided many constructive comments and suggestions, they did not see the final draft of the workshop summary before its release. The review of this workshop summary was overseen by **RON ACKERMANN,** Indiana University. Appointed by the Institute of Medicine, he was responsible for making certain that an independent examination of this workshop summary was carried out in accordance with institutional procedures and that all review comments were carefully considered. Responsibility for the final content of this workshop summary rests entirely with the rapporteurs and the institution.

Contents

1   INTRODUCTION   1
Overview, 4
Personal Testimonies, 6
Organization of Workshop Summary, 6

2   HOME HEALTH CARE: TODAY AND TOMORROW   11
Current State of Home Health Care, 11
Home Health Care 2024: The Ideal State, 16

3   TOWARD PERSONAL HEALTH: GOING HOME AND
    BEYOND   23
Taking Control—At Home, 23
Lessons from Japan and China, 25
From Mainframe to Personal Health, 27
Pillars of Personal Health, 30
Principles for the Evolution of Health Care, 32
Questions and Comments, 33

4   KEY ISSUES AND TRENDS   35
Trends in Population Health, 35
Trends in Public Policy, 40
Trends in the Real World, 41
Questions and Comments, 44

5   THE HOME HEALTH CARE WORKFORCE   49
    The Value of Team-Based Care, 49
    Supporting Families, 56
    Direct Care Workers, 57
    Care Coordination and the Consumer Voice, 61
    Questions and Comments, 62

6   MODELS OF CARE AND APPROACHES TO PAYMENT   65
    Overview of the Range of Models and Approaches to Payment, 65
    Experience of Sutter Health, 72
    Experience of Atrius Health, 74
    Experience of the Visiting Nurse Service of New York, 77
    Experience of Humana At Home, 79
    Experience of Optum Complex Population Management, 82
    Experience of the CAPABLE Model, 84
    Questions and Comments, 86

7   INNOVATIONS IN TECHNOLOGY   91
    Evidence Base for Home Health Care Technologies, 91
    Role of Telehealth, 95
    Use and Development of Assistive Technology, 97
    Questions and Comments, 100

8   MAKING CONNECTIONS   105
    Connecting to the Larger Health Care Ecosystem, 105
    MediCaring Accountable Care Communities: Connecting Health
        Care and Social Services, 109
    Connecting the Data, 111
    Questions and Comments, 115

9   REFLECTIONS AND REACTIONS   117
    Reflections on Day One, 117
    Final Reactors Panel, 121
    Final Thoughts from Workshop Participants, 127

REFERENCES   129

APPENDIXES

A   WORKSHOP AGENDA   131
B   SPEAKER AND MODERATOR BIOGRAPHICAL SKETCHES   137

1

Introduction[1]

A 2011 report by the National Research Council (NRC) declared, "Health care is coming home" (NRC, 2011, p. 9). The report further noted that although the costs of care are one driver of this change, the delivery of health care at home is valued by individuals and can promote healthy living and well-being when it is managed well. Living independently at home is a priority for many, especially individuals who are aging with or into disability. However, both the complexity and the intensity of the health care services provided in home settings are increasing.

Additionally, individuals with disabilities, chronic conditions, and functional impairments need a range of services and supports to keep living independently. However, there often is not a strong link between medical care provided in the home and the necessary social services and supports for independent living. Home health agencies and others are rising to the challenges of meeting the needs and demands of these populations to stay at home by exploring alternative models of care and payment approaches, the best use of their workforces, and technologies that can enhance independent living. All of these challenges and opportunities lead to the consideration of how home health care fits into the future health care system overall.

On September 30 and October 1, 2014, the Institute of Medicine

---

[1] The planning committee's role was limited to planning the workshop, and the workshop summary has been prepared by the workshop rapporteurs as a factual summary of what occurred at the workshop. Statements, recommendations, and opinions expressed are those of the individual presenters and participants and are not necessarily endorsed or verified by the IOM or the NRC, and they should not be construed as reflecting any group consensus.

(IOM) and the NRC convened a public workshop on the future of home health care. The workshop was supported by a group of sponsors (see p. ii of this workshop summary) and hosted by the IOM-NRC Forum on Aging, Disability, and Independence,[2] an ongoing neutral venue in which stakeholders in government, academia, industry, philanthropic organizations, and consumer groups meet to discuss the intersection of aging and disability. The workshop itself was planned by an ad hoc committee. (See Box 1-1 for the committee's statement of task.) Under the NRC guidelines, workshops are designed as convening activities and do not result in any formal findings, conclusions, or recommendations. Furthermore, the workshop summary reflects what transpired at the workshop and does not present any consensus views of either the planning committee or workshop participants. The purpose of this summary is to capture important points raised by the individual speakers and workshop participants. A webcast of the workshop is also available.[3]

The workshop brought together stakeholders from a spectrum of public and private organizations and thought leaders for discussions to improve their understanding of the current and potential future role of home health care in supporting aging in place and in helping high-risk adults (particularly older adults) with chronic illnesses and disabilities to receive health care and long-term services and supports (LTSS)[4] in their homes and avoid potentially higher-cost, institution-based care. The workshop planners were especially interested in evaluating how home health care fits into evolving models of health care delivery and payment resulting from the Patient Protection and Affordable Care Act of 2010[5] and other policies, including those resulting from potential changes in the Medicare home health care benefit (which was designed nearly 50 years ago). In addition, the workshop sought to explore the key policy reforms and investments in workforces, technologies, and research that will be needed to maximize the value of home health care and to describe the ways in which research can help clarify the value of these services.

In this workshop, as in other settings, terms such as home health care, home health, home health services, home care, home-based care, and other

---

[2] See www.iom.edu/ADIForum (accessed December 5, 2014).

[3] See http://www.iom.edu/activities/aging/futurehomehealthcare/2014-sep-30.aspx (accessed December 24, 2014).

[4] "Long-term services and supports" are also referred to as "long-term care," but the former term is now preferred as a more accurate and comprehensive description of the kinds of assistance needed by people with disabilities. This workshop summary generally uses the term LTSS, but it refers to long-term care in contexts in which the term has become standard, such as long-term care facilities or long-term care insurance.

[5] Patient Protection and Affordable Care Act of 2010, Public Law 111-148, 111th Cong., 2nd sess. (March 23, 2010).

BOX 1-1
Statement of Task

An ad hoc committee will plan a 2-day public workshop, bringing together a spectrum of public and private stakeholders and thought leaders to improve understanding of (1) the current role of Medicare home health care in supporting aging in place and in helping high-risk, chronically ill, and disabled Americans receive health care in their communities; (2) the evolving role of Medicare home health care in caring for Americans in the future, including how to integrate Medicare home health care into new models for the delivery of care and the future health care marketplace; (3) the key policy reforms and investments in workforces, technologies, and research needed to leverage the value of home health care to support older Americans; and (4) research priorities that can help clarify the value of home health care.

The workshop will feature invited presentations and discussions that will

1. Provide an overview of the current state of home health care, including the relevance of Medicare-certified home health agencies in supporting community-based care and healthy aging in place, and an understanding of current barriers to home health care (e.g., budgetary constraints, definitions, practice-level restrictions, and the absence of meaningful use incentives);
2. Inform understanding of the evolving role of Medicare home health care and its role in the future by examining and exploring innovative models for the delivery of care that involve Medicare-certified home health agencies, home health care professionals, and other aspects of health care at home to achieve the triple aim of improving the patient experience of care (including quality and satisfaction), improving the health of populations, and reducing the per capita cost of health care; and
3. Inform understanding of how to facilitate the future role of home health care in achieving the triple aim by examining and exploring

   a. The infrastructure needs for home health care, the health care system as a whole, and the overall environment;
   b. The workforce needs, that is, the supply of professionals that are educated and trained to deliver home health care;
   c. The research and measurement needs for home health care to provide high-quality and efficient care and to allow healthy aging;
   d. The technology needs (including mobile, digital, monitoring, health information, therapeutic, and diagnostic needs) to enable and support the health care of patients at home; and
   e. The policy reforms (including funding and accountable care considerations) and communications strategies needed to recognize the value of home health care and the importance of home health care professionals as part of a comprehensive health care team.

similar terms were often used interchangeably, and with various intended meanings. In some instances, workshop speakers and participants implied a more strict interpretation of home health care (and other similar terms) as including only medical services or in reference to the Medicare home health care benefit only, whereas other speakers and participants spoke to home health care as more inclusive of a variety of services and supports provided in the home. This summary uses the term *home health care* for consistency (except in cases of direct quotes), recognizing that each speaker or participant may have intended a different spectrum of care. Where possible, the spectrum intended by the speaker is noted. In addition, although the statement of task (see Box 1-1) called for a focus on the Medicare home health care benefit, the workshop planners encouraged all speakers to also consider home health care broadly—that is, more than just medical services and more than just the Medicare benefit. As a result, some workshop speakers focused primarily on Medicare home health care, but many other topics included under a broader definition of home health care were also discussed, to varying degrees.

OVERVIEW

Workshop participants were welcomed by planning committee co-chairs Bruce Leff, Johns Hopkins University School of Medicine, and Elizabeth Madigan, Frances Payne Bolton School of Nursing, Case Western Reserve University, who began with an overview of home health care across the spectrum of services and supports (see Figure 1-1).

Moving from left to right, Figure 1-1 shows that this spectrum ranges from care for lower-acuity levels care to higher acuity, and from chronic care to more acute care. It also moves from models in which there is little or no medical doctor (MD) involvement in the home toward models in which MD involvement is substantial. The figure shows that this spectrum starts with informal care services provided at home, often by family members—typically, daughters, spouses, or daughters-in-law, Leff said. Estimates suggest that somewhere between 10 million and 15 million people currently receive such care in the home.

Next, moving right, is formal personal care services—that is, paid-for services—for people who need additional help or who do not have family at home to help them. An estimated 2 million Americans receive these formal personal care services, Leff said. Next is Medicare skilled home health care, which is used for post-acute care, as well as for people in the community who are homebound, according to the definitions of Medicare, and have skilled home health care needs (which was a focus of the discussion over the 2 days of the workshop). More than 3 million Medicare recipients use those services. Farther to the right is home-based primary care, which

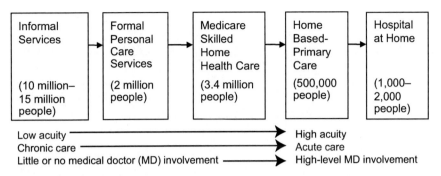

FIGURE 1-1 Home health care across the spectrum of services and supports, including numbers of individuals receiving care.
SOURCE: Reprinted with permission from Bruce Leff and Elizabeth Madigan, 2014.

involves physicians, nurse practitioners, or physician assistants providing longitudinal medical care, which is often team-based care and which is often provided in collaboration with social services providers to a population that is essentially homebound. Leff said that an estimated 500,000 people receive these services, acknowledging that this number "is the most back-of-the-envelope calculation" of the array. Finally, on the far right of Figure 1-1 are acute-care, hospital-level services provided in the home, including care provided through hospital-at-home-type models, such as the model developed by the Johns Hopkins Schools of Medicine and Public Health.[6] To date, many fewer people receive these more intensive home-based services, although the workshop discussion suggested that the trend is for more and more people to receive such services.

Leff noted that the move from left to right in Figure 1-1 entails a move from the provision of health care services to individuals with lower-acuity levels of need to individuals with higher-acuity ones requiring a mix of acute and chronic care services and, finally, to the provision of acute care in the home. It also moves from models with little or no physician or medical involvement to those in which medical involvement is substantial, Leff said.

The four principal factors driving the development and use of these spectrum-of-care approaches are policy, payment, technology, and demographics, Madigan said. Much attention is paid to the last factor, "as we anticipate the aging of the American population, the projected increase in the number of people with multiple chronic conditions or functional impairments, and the impact that's going to have on the health care system,"

---

[6] See http://www.hospitalathome.org (accessed December 24, 2014).

she said. Moreover, that growth is a constant, whereas the other factors—policy, payment, and technology—are amenable to change.

The current array of chronic care and home-based services is not well integrated, Madigan argued. Payments and some of the care providers are in separate silos. "From a patient's perspective, you can have multiple agencies providing services, and they don't know about each other or who is doing what piece [of the care]," Madigan said. In a true system of home health care, she said, services would be integrated and those providing these services would provide care along a continuum that would involve collaborations with partners in the community as well as those in facility-based long-term care, because patients often end up there at least for short periods, before going home again and receiving home health care services. In other words, across the spectrum of care, from informal services to the hospital in the home, what is needed is a focus "on what the patient needs and how we can help provide that in a seamless way," said Madigan.

PERSONAL TESTIMONIES

Personal testimony on caring for family members at home was presented by James Martinez from Oakland, California (see Box 1-2), and Karen Marshall, Kadamba Tree Foundation, Washington, DC (see Box 1-3).[7] Although their experiences with home health care are different, their stories present two perspectives on some of the strengths and shortcomings of the current system of provision of health care in the home.

ORGANIZATION OF WORKSHOP SUMMARY

This workshop summary is limited to describing the presentations given and the general topics discussed during the workshop itself. Overall, each speaker's presentation is captured in a section attributed to that individual. All of the workshop discussions with the audience have also been captured in a variety of ways. In some cases, the topics raised and the responses given during the discussion periods are incorporated into the section describing the speaker's presentation. In other cases in which a new topic or line of discussion arose, a separate section describing the new topic is introduced at the end of the chapter. Comments made by workshop participants were attributed to the individuals by name when possible. (If identification of the speaker was not possible, the individual is referred to as a "workshop

---

[7] To watch these testimonies on video, see http://www.iom.edu/Activities/Aging/FutureHomeHealthCare/2014-SEP-30/Day-1/Session-1-Videos/2-Martinez-Video.aspx (accessed December 24, 2014) and http://www.iom.edu/Activities/Aging/FutureHomeHealthCare/2014-SEP-30/Day-2/Overview/32-Marshall-Video.aspx (accessed December 24, 2014).

BOX 1-2
James Martinez's Story

Home health was all new to me in 2011, when my mom was diagnosed with pancreatic cancer. She did not want to stay at home, because she didn't have any health care there. I told her that if they would teach me what to do, I would take her home and I would take care of her until she passed. And it turned out, it was way better with home care than with the hospital. I was always at odds with the staff at the hospital.

So that's what happened, with the support of the Sutter Home Care people up through hospice services, and they were there for me also, with the bereavement. They never left my side.

The following year, my dad got sick. I moved out of my house at that point and moved in with him, because he needed full-time care. I took care of him until May of this year. I couldn't have done it without help, giving morphine and all these other drugs, knowing when to do it, and how to do it. I would call them, and I had just terrific telesupport. They'd call me back in 15 minutes, and if the drugs hadn't worked, they would send out a nurse.

They showed me how to do everything. With my mom, I had to clean and change and administer the medicines through a PICC (peripherally inserted central catheter) line. With my dad, he had a nebulizer. He had air. They explained the equipment, so there were no questions, really.

Sutter took care of me, too. They came with a social worker and a nurse. The nurse would take care of my dad and do his vitals and all that and talk with him. The social worker would come into the kitchen with me, and we would sit and talk about me: how I can take care of myself, what I needed, because they said if I couldn't be healthy, I couldn't take care of him.

I didn't have any help from any of my other family members. And I was trying to work and trying to do everything else that needed to be done around the house. Eventually, I had to quit my job. My dad's retirement income was too much, so we weren't eligible for me to be paid for his home care. If there was one thing that could change, it would be to give a little bit more financial help to the family.

I'm not the only one who's done this. There are a lot of people. There's a neighbor down the street. His dad passed away, and he took care of him. The two of us would talk and get a little bit of strength from each other.

SOURCE: Presentation by James Martinez, September 30, 2014.

---

participant.") Presentations are also not necessarily organized in the same order in which they occurred at the actual workshop but have been rearranged to provide a better flow for the readers of this workshop summary.

Chapter 2 presents two keynote addresses (by Robert J. Rosati and Steven Landers, both of whom are with the Visiting Nurse Association Health Group) that address the current state of home health care overall

BOX 1-3
Karen Marshall's Story

Karen Marshall began her presentation by quoting former First Lady Rosalynn Carter[a]:

There are only four types of people in this world:
Those who have been caregivers,
Those who are currently caregivers,
Those who will be caregivers, and
Those who will need a caregiver.

I must say, I wake up every morning and think about that quote. For the past 10 years, family caregiving has been a big part of my life. Like Mr. Martinez, I'm a repeat caregiver. I first cared for my mother, who had cancer. And a couple of months after she died, my father developed a heart problem. He was in his late 70s at the time and had never had any health problems. I suspect his heart broke, because along with me he was a caregiver for my mom.

That series of events really changed the trajectory of my life and how I think about caregiving, even though it has been a part of my life since I was a baby. My grandfather came to live with us when I was just a baby. His aging process took the same trajectory as many of the people in the rural neighborhood I grew up in, and when he was no longer able to stay home, he went to live with his daughter, my mother, who took care of him while she raised me. And when that was no longer feasible, he went into a nursing home.

Fast forward 20 years, and when I was in college, my grandmother had a stroke. My family helped her stay at home as long as possible, and eventually she moved in with us. While I was home for the summer, my mother and I split caregiving duties. A home health agency sent an aide to stay with her while we were at work. I only remember one agency at the time, which served a pretty broad multicounty area. That experience shaped how my family felt about home health care for a while, and it wasn't necessarily a positive experience. It helped in that we could continue to work, but we were concerned about the skill and the quality of the care, and from others in the community, we heard stories about fraud and abuse.

Fast forward another 10 years, when my mother got sick in her early 60s. She was just 61 when she passed away, and her care at home was private pay. She did have private insurance. It helped that I could take a leave of absence from my job to help care for her in the last couple of months. At the time, I was an attorney here in DC, right on K Street, in a large firm. That's when my perception of home health care began to shift, because the last time she was discharged from the hospital we knew she was going home to die. It was very comforting for my family to have the help of hospice. They set up the hospital bed in the bedroom. The nurse and caseworker really helped me understand what was going on and recognize the signs of her decline.

A couple of months after her death my father got sick. I did not see that coming. I was still winding down my mom's estate. I was returning to work when my father became ill, and it never really crossed our minds what would happen after he left the hospital. Part of the reason for that is that my big sister is a registered nurse, and she was able to take him home with her. He stayed with her several weeks until he went back to his own home, but he'd lost so much of his independence—a lot of his life. He was a logger, and up until his mid- to late 70s, he was going out into the woods chopping down trees every day. He'd lost his health, which he had always had, and his strength, which he had always prided himself on, and he had lost his spouse.

We did our best for several years to help him stay at home, which was his wish. In retrospect, it would've helped us tremendously to look at the home health care options. My dad was a little particular about how he wanted to be cared for, and we didn't want to disrupt his expectations that much. But it became a burden to me. It was not uncommon for me to come out of a meeting to a voicemail that my dad was on his way to the emergency room, a 4-hour drive away. I went home every weekend for a long time and eventually cut back to several times a month.

It just became too difficult to juggle all these responsibilities, and eventually, in 2009, I left my job. The financial repercussions of that choice continue to this day. At the time I was married; I'm not anymore. I don't regret my decision, but in retrospect I would have made different choices, especially given all that I now know—and have witnessed—about the options that home health care provides. Earlier this year my father was diagnosed with dementia.

This time we are relying on home health care. We have no choice. My sister has been on medical leave herself and can't take additional time off. And I am just not in a position to stop working again. So we ended up relying on a home health agency to send in aides 24/7, which was not a long-term solution, as it cost us about $400 a day. We were applying for Medicaid benefits, and he primarily received his health care from the VA [the U.S. Department of Veterans Affairs], which was a great help. This financial assistance came through at just the right time, but still, the expenses were enormous.

I would go down there a few days every week. This was a difficult time for him, because he was coming to grips with his diagnosis and having me in and out was not necessarily the most comforting thing, which upset me because I was used to being of some comfort to him. The home health aides provided continuity. He got to know and like them. It helped to know I had eyes and ears to not only look after his medical situation but also his well-being in other ways.

Two social workers from our local Program of All-Inclusive Care for the Elderly (PACE) came in and did an evaluation, and they had an honest conversation with us about our options. They explained that it just wasn't safe for him at home. We couldn't guarantee that a health worker would always be around. This helped us feel better about a tough decision that we had to make. I still struggle a bit with that. I feel bad that after all of this effort: leaving my job, all the trips up and down I-95. Ultimately, his wish of being able to stay at home couldn't come true. But every time I see him now he looks healthier. His medication is being managed properly. He's gained his weight back. He smiles and he's happy. And he's not scared anymore. I really do credit home health care for helping us cross that bridge.

continued

BOX 1-3 Continued

I would probably add a fifth person to First Lady Rosalynn Carter's scenario of caregivers. I would add people who have to work with the caregiver. And that would include my former boss, who was very sad to see me go. That would include my coworkers, who had to pick up the slack on the days when I had to head down I-95 to an emergency room. That would include the health care professionals who had to tell us about my dad's diagnosis while he was sitting there in the room. It would include the social workers who had to break the news to us about how difficult honoring my dad's wish would be.

[a] See the remarks of Rosalynn Carter at http://gos.sbc.edu/c/carter.html (accessed December 24, 2014).
SOURCE: Presented by Karen Marshall, October 1, 2014.

and changes occurring in the field, as well as an exploration of the future ideal state of home health care. Chapter 3 presents a keynote address by Eric Dishman of Intel on the role of home health care in achieving his vision of personal health. Chapter 4 examines the key issues and trends currently framing the discussion of home health care, such as trends in population health and public policy. The next several chapters explore the health care workforce (Chapter 5), the models of care and approaches to payment (Chapter 6), and the technology (Chapter 7) needed to reach the ideal state of home health care. Chapter 8 considers how home health care can be linked to the broader health care system, to communities, and to larger data systems. Finally, Chapter 9 provides reflections and reactions to the 2-day workshop from the perspectives of the moderators of the two panels on workforce and models of care and payment approaches on the first day of the workshop, from the perspectives of individuals who presented their reactions to the workshop presentations over both days of the workshop, and lastly, from the perspectives of the individual workshop participants, who described their own takeaways from the workshop.

2

Home Health Care: Today and Tomorrow

During the workshop, two keynote speakers addressed the state of home health care to provide a framework for the workshop discussions. Robert J. Rosati of the Visiting Nurse Association (VNA) Health Group gave a broad overview of the current state of home health care. Later, after a panel on some of the key issues and trends affecting home health care planning (see Chapter 4), Steven Landers, also of VNA Health Group, gave his vision for the ideal state of home health care 10 years from now.

CURRENT STATE OF HOME HEALTH CARE

Robert J. Rosati
Visiting Nurse Association Health Group

Rosati summarized the current state of home health care, with a focus on Medicare home health care, and the changes occurring in the field to provide context for discussions about the challenges and opportunities of home health care in the future.

The Medicare Population

Population trends are driving the shape and scope of home health care services. Most people enrolled in Medicare today have three or more chronic conditions (65 percent), half live below the poverty line, nearly one-third (31 percent) have a cognitive or mental impairment, and about 5 percent live in long-term care facilities (Kaiser Family Foundation, 2014).

In addition, although the tendency is to lump the Medicare population into one group, about 16 percent of Medicare enrollees are individuals with disabilities younger than the age of 65 years and 13 percent are aged 85 years and older. In addition to these challenges, Medicare beneficiaries are often in fair or poor health, according to self-ratings, and have two or more problems with activities of daily living (ADLs).[1]

Rosati illustrated the growth in the size of this population by comparing the numbers of Americans age 65 years and older in 2002 (35.5 million) and 2012 (43.1 million). Estimates for 2040 are that some 80 million Americans will be age 65 years and older, and about 29 million of those individuals will have some degree of disability. Meanwhile, the number of Americans ages 85 years and older is projected to grow from 5.9 million today to about 14.1 million in 2040, he said.

The number of agencies providing home health care in the United States grew from 8,314 in 2005 to 12,613 in 2013, Rosati said, with Medicare expenditures for home health care services nearly doubling from 9.7 billion in 2001 to about $18.3 billion in 2012. Nevertheless, home health care constitutes only about 3 percent of Medicare benefits payments.

The Medicare Home Health Care Program

People who are recognized as needing home health care are those who have had a recent hospitalization or those who have received a physician referral. Rosati offered several key points about eligibility for the Medicare home health services:

- The recipient must be under the care of a physician who has established a plan of care for the patient (a requirement over which the home health agency does not have control);
- The care plan must include the need for nursing care or physical, speech, or occupational therapy;
- The recipient must obtain care through a Medicare-certified home health agency; and
- The recipient must be homebound and unable to leave the home unaided without the possibility of risk.

Two major assumptions underlie these eligibility criteria, Rosati said: that the physician drives the care and that the patient has certain needs (from a clinical perspective and because he or she is homebound).

Further, Rosati added, if a beneficiary needs skilled nursing care, that

---

[1] ADLs are the routine tasks of everyday life, such as eating, bathing, dressing, using the toilet, transferring (e.g., from a bed to a chair), and walking across a room.

care must be needed only intermittently or part-time and must be provided by a registered nurse (RN) or a licensed practice nurse supervised by an RN. Home health aide services must supplement the care provided by professionals. Additional services that may be provided include medical social services and medical supplies. Said Rosati, "What's important to look at is what's not covered." Services that are not covered include 24-hour care, meals, homemaker services, and personal care not associated with therapy or nursing. In some states, however, Medicaid does cover these services for low-income residents.

Medicare beneficiaries receive skilled care in the home on an episodic basis. The skilled care is certified for a certain period of time—typically, 60 days—and skilled care can be renewed if the beneficiary needs such care for a longer period, Rosati said. In contrast, Rosati, said, commercial insurers typically authorize a certain number of visits (5 or 10, for example).

Unskilled services help people safely stay in their own home for the longest period of time, and although these services are not covered by Medicare's home health care program, they may be covered in other ways or paid for out-of-pocket. A notable model of comprehensive noninstitutional care is the Program of All-Inclusive Care for the Elderly (PACE), a program jointly funded by Medicare and Medicaid that provides an integrated set of services at a PACE center in the community, with some home health care support, for nursing home-eligible recipients.[2]

Quality Measures

National home health care quality measures compiled for the Centers for Medicare & Medicaid Services' Home Health Compare website suggest that home health agencies provide high-quality services according to key process measures, Rosati said, with home health agencies providing:

- Checks for depression and the risk of falls 98 percent of the time,
- Instructions to family members 93 percent of the time, and
- Timely initiation of patient care 92 percent of the time.

The average performance is somewhat lower for health outcome measures, which, in part, reflects the debility of people who need home health care, Rosati said. For example, some performance measures indicate:

- Postsurgical wound improvement or healing 89 percent of the time,
- Reduction of pain when moving around 68 percent of the time,

---

[2] See http://www.npaonline.org/website/article.asp?id=12&title=Who,_What_and_Where_Is_PACE (accessed December 24, 2014).

- Improvement in walking or moving around 62 percent of the time, and
- Readmission to the hospital within 60 days 16 percent of the time.

Rosati noted that the home health care field, on average, is achieving the same readmission rates as hospitals, although, he noted, the hospital readmission rate is calculated only on the basis of hospital readmission in the first 30 days after the patient is released and, therefore, is somewhat easier to achieve.

Finally, how do beneficiaries themselves rate the home health care services that they have received? Again, using national averages from Home Health Compare, Rosati reported that

- Seventy-nine percent of patients say that they would definitely recommend their home health care agency to friends and family (whereas 71 percent would recommend their hospital);
- Eighty-four percent gave the overall care that they received from the home health care agency a rating of 9 or 10 on a 10-point scale;
- Eighty-four percent reported that the home health care team discussed medicine, pain, and home safety with them; and
- Eighty-five percent said that the home health care team communicated well.

Reimbursement

In recent years, the federal government has cut Medicare reimbursement for home health care services, and in the near future, another $25 billion "will be taken out of the home health care system," Rosati said. Another source of cuts has resulted from states' moves to managed long-term care for Medicaid recipients, which has curtailed the number of hours of patient care provided in the home. Additional reductions in commercial payers' reimbursements, as well as in Medicare Advantage, Medicare's managed care program, have occurred.

Further financial challenges result from the high level of scrutiny and auditing to which home health agencies are subjected, which have resulted in part from fraud and abuse in the system. Good organizations, Rosati said, "are kind of trapped with respect to what's being said about other organizations."

Emerging Innovations

Home health care providers are involved with a number of emerging models that organize and pay for care differently. Among them are innovations that were established under the Patient Protection and Affordable Care Act of 2010 (ACA),[3] such as accountable care organizations (ACOs) and bundled payment arrangements. Specifically, Rosati said,

- Home health care organizations are finding opportunities to work directly with ACOs to deliver community-based care.
- Home health care organizations are involved with the provision of post-acute care services that involve the use of both home health care and skilled nursing to provide the right level of care after hospitalization.
- Increasingly, home health care organizations are involved with transitional care, in which their first visit to the patient is in the hospital and then they make perhaps one visit after the patient is discharged.
- Home health care organizations' patient assessment skills and experience working in the home are being tapped for evaluations of high-risk enrollees in health plans.

The challenge is to cover the cost of these service expansions, Rosati said. The infrastructure of home health agencies has been built around Medicare, and these new arrangements require agencies to operate differently. Everything from software systems to care delivery models need to be redesigned, and mind sets need to be adjusted, he said. Furthermore, competition in these emerging arenas is significant: "Everybody wants to be in this space right now," Rosati said. Coordination among the various entities providing transitional care—the hospital, the insurance company, and others—is not easily achieved, however.

For some time, even though home health care has tended to use electronic records for both the collection of clinical information and assessment, meaningful use provisions under the ACA do not apply to long-term care. Home health care also has not benefited from the exchange of clinical data with other providers, nor do home health agencies have the patient portals that hospitals are required to provide their patients. Larger home health agencies are paying close attention to reporting and analysis of quality outcomes, but smaller ones have trouble paying for data analysis expertise and electronic records systems.

Finally, telehealth applications (e.g., video, remote monitoring, automated calls) have been found to be effective and cost-effective by some organizations. However, no additional reimbursement is provided for the development and use of telehealth, a deficiency that is curtailing movement

---

[3] Patient Protection and Affordable Care Act of 2010, Public Law 111-148, 111th Cong., 2nd sess. (March 23, 2010).

in this area, Rosati said. Expansion of telehealth may first need to occur with younger populations or those more comfortable with this technology, he suggested, reserving nurse visits for those who are not as comfortable with its use. Howeverm telehealth can be low-tech, involving no more than regular calls to the family.

In summary, Rosati stated,

- The demand for community-based care will grow substantially;
- Patients and families prefer care at home;
- The home is the least costly setting for post-acute, long-term care; and
- Home health agencies have the experience, knowledge, and infrastructure needed to support emerging models of the delivery of health care.

HOME HEALTH CARE 2024: THE IDEAL STATE

Steven Landers
Visiting Nurse Association Health Group

VNA Health Group, which Steven Landers leads, is a large nonprofit home health care, hospice, and community health care organization started more than 100 years ago by Geraldine Thompson with the support of her lifelong friend, Eleanor Roosevelt. Predicting the future of home health care is a risky endeavor, but "for this workshop, let's assume the future state is up to us," Landers said, emphasizing the importance of the task.

Advantages of Home-Based Care

Home health care offers some basic, commonsense advantages within the continuum of health care that are as real today as when Lillian Wald and her colleagues ventured into the squalor of New York's Lower East Side at the end of the 19th century, Landers said. These advantages include

- An enhanced view of patients and caregivers that leads to a better understanding of important issues, like how they manage medications and nutrition;
- Access to health care that is most relevant to patients with physical and socioeconomic barriers to care;
- A more intimate clinician–patient relationship "around the kitchen table," as Barbara A. McCann of Interim HealthCare said in the workshop (see Chapter 4);

- Clinician expression of an act of humility that demonstrates that clinicians have left their comfort zone to be on their patients' turf and that the patient and family are worth being truly known and visited;
- Lower costs for services that are desired more by many patients; and
- Sometimes, greater safety for frail elders, because they will have fewer of the common complications of hospitalization, such as delirium.

Because of these advantages, the home and community will emerge in the future as the main settings for a myriad of health care services, he said, adding that "the home setting and health services and supports will become so synonymous that they may not be called home care; rather, they will just be modern health care."

Home-centered care is centered on the patient, offering holistic, sophisticated, and individualized care at home for people with serious and disabling conditions. Landers believes that home-centered care will grow into a major national strategy for the provision of health care because its benefits for both payers and patients are so powerful. Nevertheless, different areas of the country will accomplish this differently and along different timelines, he said, and the purchasers and organizers of care may vary from one place to another.

Meeting the Care Mission

Landers said that within the context of Medicare, the mission of home health care is to

- Help beneficiaries, especially patients with lower levels of mobility, safely transition to home from hospitals and facilities and continue their recovery and rehabilitation at home, and
- Help the highest-risk chronically ill beneficiaries age in place in home and community settings both by meeting certain primary medical care needs and by intermittently escalating the care provided at home to avoid the need for hospitalization. Aging in place in the home includes efforts to help beneficiaries remain comfortable at home in the last 6 to 12 months of life.

Emerging trends in the health care system will accelerate strategies to provide post-acute care in the home, he said. Electronic information exchange among providers and other technologies will improve the patient and family experience and ensure the use of home health care services at the appropriate intensity. In addition, transitional care models that include posthospitalization home health care visits will become commonplace for many more people than are now eligible for them.

For high-risk chronically ill people, organizations like Independence at Home[4] practices, patient-centered medical homes, and models of care for advanced illness will partner with home health agencies and community resources to reduce the amount of time patients spend in hospitals and nursing homes, improve key indicators of well-being for patients and caregivers, use technology to improve the home health care experience, and greatly increase the proportion of the oldest old who die at home with hospice care.

Ingredients for Progress

Four main ingredients will be needed to effect this evolution and can be put in place by all varieties of payers and organizations:

- Development and oversight of interdisciplinary home health care plans by physicians and advanced practice nurses informed by proven concepts of holistic geriatric medicine, palliative medicine, and rehabilitation medicine;
- Enhanced support during care transitions that addresses self-management, care coordination, information transfer, and clinical stabilization;
- An advanced capability for escalating the intensity of medical and palliative care at home in times of decline or exacerbation of a patient's illness or medical condition (including escalation to hospital-like services at home); and
- The thoughtful use of advanced information technology between encounters to aid with the management of problems that arise between visits and to improve triage and the overall efficiency of care.

According to Landers, the single most important issue determining whether the potential of home-centered care is realized and the pace at which it will be realized is the strength of the nation's Medicare-certified home health agencies. These organizations exist in virtually every community; employ hundreds of thousands of staff who are nurses, therapists, other clinicians, and aides; make more than 100 million home visits per year; and collectively, have many strong community ties. "I view many of these agencies as local and national treasures that should be improved,

---

[4] See http://www.iahnow.com (accessed December 24, 2014).

not torn down," he said. He noted, however, problems with the current licensure and accreditation framework and the imperfect payment model.

A set of policies that would support the home health care infrastructure and help it play the role that Landers envisions would

- Tie payments to outcomes and experience and facilitate provider participation in a diverse range of alternative payment models;
- Enable the hiring of medical directors (who would, for example, link home health care to the services offered by other key providers);
- Have interdisciplinary team case reviews, similar to the approach used by hospices;
- Make the interventions used during the transition of care a covered home health care service, irrespective of whether a patient is homebound;
- Facilitate technology upgrades to improve the flow of information among providers and between home health agencies and the patients and families served; and
- Develop training and careers for agency staff in state-of-the-art geriatric, palliative, and rehabilitation medicine, as well as in strategies for the coordination of care.

This central role would be further aided, he said, "by making major fraud and abuse concerns a thing of the past." In the future, home health agencies should be accredited not just at the time of licensure but on an ongoing basis. Selected utilization metrics should be publicly reported. Value-based purchasing and oversight models should reduce variability across agencies, and efforts should be made to weed out less capable entities. If this were done, even the Medicare-certified home health agency of 2024 with the lowest level of performance would be "a serious and skilled clinical organization with the talent, culture, and technology [required] to be a core part of helping physicians and advanced practice nurses address Medicare cost and quality challenges."

The best models and approaches and the resources and policies needed for success will be identified over time, and Landers offered the following advice for going forward:

> As we explore these different models, let's try to minimize the importance of the names and labels; where there are common home-centered themes and resources that can help, we should elevate those ideas irrespective of the packaging. We should avoid the temptation of trying to pick winners and losers between marginally different concepts whose success is more dependent on local execution. Instead, let's focus on how we can ensure

that all of these well-intended and reasonably conceived efforts at advancing home-centered care are as successful as possible.

In conclusion, he said, "a bright home-centered health system is clearly and tangibly before us if we continue to nurture the seeds of change that are starting to grow, while taking steps to optimize rather than diminish our home health agencies."

Questions and Comments

An open discussion followed Landers's presentation. Workshop participants were able to give comments and ask questions. The following section summarizes the discussion session.

Bruce Leff, Johns Hopkins University, asked Landers about the decreasing emphasis on medical services and the creation of stronger links to social services. Landers indicated that he recognizes the importance of both medical and social supports but stated that Medicare is essentially a medical services program and not a long-term care system and that he would not advocate for it to become one. He also said that medical providers should take a biopsychosocial approach to the provision of their medical care and should make efforts to assess and coordinate social supports in high-risk situations. Furthermore, Landers said, if people are going to age in place at home with long-term services and supports, they will need both primary medical services and other types of supporting services, only some of which are covered under current Medicare rules.

In response to a question from a workshop participant on the role of the individual, Landers said that care starts with medical care based on evidence-based geriatric medicine, palliative medicine, and rehabilitation medicine, all of which take a patient-centered approach using a comprehensive biopsychosocial assessment and a multifaceted model for the planning of care. At the same time, he said, some of the population groups that would benefit the most from home health care are quite dependent, as a result of impairment in cognitive function and an inability to perform activities of daily living. Landers explained that in these situations health policy makers should still develop programs that respect the individual but should be vigilant that some individuals are so impaired that the risk of neglect and suffering without aggressive intervention is high.

Penny Feldman, Visiting Nurse Service of New York, asked Landers to indicate the one or two most important actions that home health agencies can take if they want to survive in the current environment. She also wanted to know in what ways organizations representing home health agencies can help them prepare to be vibrant agencies in the future. Landers said that home health agencies need to embrace the role of value creation. Home health agency staff sometimes say, "these hospitals don't know what they're doing. They send these patients home that are so sick. They have all these needs. They're complicated. What were they thinking?" Actually, Landers said, these are exactly the situations in which home health agencies have the most opportunity to create value. Their value cannot be established on the basis of the provision of marginal services but can be established on the basis of the provision of services that produce health and cost outcomes that are different from those that they would otherwise be without home health care. A second benefit of acquiring an attitude of value, he said, would be to eliminate efforts to manipulate the system, for example, making an extra visit to obtain additional reimbursement. This speaks to the parallel need for a culture of accountability in places where it does not exist today.

Feldman further asked if anything in the existing Medicare home health care benefit could help home health agencies have greater flexibility and even with their survival. At the national level, Landers said, the development of a common vision for where home health agencies need to be in the future would enable stronger advocacy for some of the policy issues. Because health care is so different from one locale to another, the vision needs to focus on broad themes and resources. In sum, he said, "What are the carrots and sticks that can get us closer to value rather than waste?"

3

Toward Personal Health: Going Home and Beyond

Eric Dishman
Intel

Dishman described his long association with the problems of the provision of health care in the patient's home and home-based primary care and the ways in which Silicon Valley–style technologies can help from his perspective as general manager of Intel's Health Strategy & Solutions Group. Despite the accomplishments with which others credit him, Dishman began by talking about what he termed his failures. "I've spent 30 years trying to take health care home and have mostly failed at doing so, because it hasn't scaled yet." These capabilities—from care models to payment models and technologies—have not become widely available to enough people.

TAKING CONTROL—AT HOME

Misdiagnosed with a rare form of kidney cancer at age 19 years, Dishman spent the next 23 years being told he would die within 1 year (until a correct diagnosis and a subsequent successful kidney transplant in 2012) and sitting in cancer clinics and dialysis clinics with people who were mostly in their 70s and 80s. As a result, he developed an interest in aging. He had the youthful "tenacity and ferocity" to try to "change the barriers that were making the experience of illness worse than it needed to be." Professionally, he began on this path studying nursing homes and two decades ago attempted a telehealth start-up for chronic care. Now he is involved in research and development at the corporate level, running a global health and life sciences business.

Three years before his cancer was diagnosed, Dishman became personally familiar with the panic that family caregivers feel when his grandmother, who had been diagnosed with Alzheimer's disease, nearly burned his grandparents' house down. He used his early-days computer to try to create an alert system ("an intelligent sensor network with remote connectivity") that would trigger when his grandmother went into the kitchen and turned on the oven in the middle of the night. Although this early experiment in the development of a technology to help seniors live independently actually failed, he said, "That was the hook. I took the bait at that moment and have never let it go." There have to be ways to change care models and use technologies to help with the exact problems that Karen Marshall mentioned (see Chapter 1, Box 1-3), he said, "and that I was experiencing back then."

His first experience with chemotherapy taught him more about asserting "consumer control." He was given a dose that was too high, and it was physically devastating. Thereafter, in 21 more rounds, he insisted that the chemotherapy be low dose, given over long periods of time, and delivered at home as much as possible.

One difficulty that Dishman has encountered is that neither paper records nor the emerging electronic health records of today include a field for patient goals. He taught his providers to use the file nickname field to insert a few words about the goals he wanted his care organized around: snow and exercise. This was to remind them that when they developed his evolving treatment plan, they were not to aim for longevity but for preserving his opportunities to ski and get exercise.

Dishman was adamant about maintaining control because over the long course of his illness he nearly died three times, each time because of system-related problems and not the cancer per se. First was the "too-much-at-once" initial chemotherapy, second was a hospital-borne infection, and third was overmedication from a care team whose members "weren't keeping track of each other." It took determination to get care provided in the way in which he wanted. As recently as 8 years ago he was told, "We can only do home care for people age 65 and above. That's all we're set up for."

The next-to-last round of chemotherapy took place at home, by self-infusion, and cost one-tenth of what a center-based procedure would have, Dishman said. He learned to operate remote patient-monitoring technologies. Yet, he says the system—from the hospital to the oncologist to the payers—fought him every step of the way. He told them, "You have the studies now, thanks to the [Institute of Medicine] and others, that show hospitals are dangerous places. I'm incredibly immune compromised, and you're insisting I continue to make the pilgrimage to the medical mainframe to do this?"

These two seeds—independent living technologies for seniors and patient-centered goals, both of which are focused on doing as much care as possible at home for as long as possible—have grown and intertwined.

LESSONS FROM JAPAN AND CHINA

In Asia, where Dishman has recently been working intensively, the need to invent home-based care models is a necessity because of the demographics of the population and other challenges. For example, Intel is helping Japanese communities that were devastated by the Fukushima earthquake and tsunami recover. Their former centralized health care services and clinical records system was destroyed. As they rebuild, Dishman said, they are working toward a home- and community-based care model that is not centralizing its capacity, technologies, and documentation.

In China, the scale of the population and the concomitant challenges can be hard to imagine. By 2020 or 2025, China will spend more than the United States on health care, Dishman said, even though they are spending far less per capita than the United States. One of the challenges in dealing with the aging population in China is the one-child family. "They now have an average couple trying to take care of four, sometimes eight people, if the great grandparents are alive." Despite a centuries-long cultural tradition of filial piety and ancestor worship, the Chinese government in 2013 joined some other countries in adopting a law saying that people had to take care of their aging parents' financial and spiritual needs.

China's growing elderly population, combined with its extreme economic challenges, "is driving some really innovative things," Dishman said. For about a decade, Intel staff have been thinking about old-age-friendly cities and the technology infrastructure that would enable such cities. A policy challenge that the Chinese face, as do many countries, is the separation of the medical care and social care sectors. The sectors need to combine their resources with private family funds to enable a team to decide in a comprehensive, flexible way what an individual or family needs most. This is in contrast to payment systems that require funds to be used in specific ways.

Analysis of the numbers of doctors and nurses in China, especially ones trained in geriatric care, stacked up against the growing need indicates such a sizable gap that it is clear that the country cannot rely on a physician- and nurse-driven model. "Most of these people will never even come close to a physician or nurse in their lifetimes," Dishman said. The country will need to adopt a community health worker–driven model that can also enlist family members and neighbors "in some pretty intensive ways." China's second big challenge is how to finance long-term care services and supports, he said. They do not have any program akin to Social Security, for example.

Intel brought in experts from around the world to demonstrate different community-based care models, focusing on the quality of the result and not the payment model or technologies employed. That exercise built Dishman's appreciation for the U.S. Department of Veterans Affairs home-based primary care program and convinced him that "the future of care is team based, collaborative, holistic, and in the community." According to Dishman, China is now trying to develop a strategy focused on creating a community care workforce, infrastructure, and business model. In truth, such a model can serve people of all ages, so the argument for it can be based on universal design principles, he said. The model that the Chinese are trying to build is a "care-flow services network" that will allow many different agencies and companies—government service providers, benefit providers, medical service providers, or family—to use a common infrastructure to deliver care in the community and, at the same time, allow substantial innovation in the applications used and services provided. They are trying to go to scale—especially to economic scale—with such a model.

The Chinese are already building smart platforms based on activities of everyday life—railway use, communications, shopping, and phones and other devices—and want to build platforms to provide services of daily living, like housing, laundry, and food, plus health management and medical services, Dishman said. They are not thinking about health care in isolation, as often happens in the United States, assuming that "everything else" is somehow taken care of. They have in mind a whole social engagement platform that includes the services needed for safe and secure living. The desire for such a comprehensive and integrated service system has emerged in Intel's ethnographic work in the 92 nations where it has studied the aging experience, he said, and in conversations with seniors, their family members, and health care professionals.

In the beginning, the Chinese envisioned a system that would be operationalized at the street level. It was difficult for the people at Intel to envision a viable entity and infrastructure at that level of the social hierarchy, but they went along with the idea for a while, finally asking, "How many older people do you have on this particular street?" When the answer came back 893,000, "street-level" organization began to make a lot of sense. Dishman, using U.S. marketing terms, said that in urban areas, the Chinese hope to "build a branded sense of identity" among all the people who live on a particular street.

In villages, in contrast, one infrastructure would serve the entire population. Indeed, part of the challenge for the Chinese in designing this comprehensive service system is dealing with the scale differences from small rural settings to medium-sized towns to the existing large cities. One approach is to start over. Some 20 new megacities that will have this old-age-friendly city infrastructure in place are being built from scratch. The national government's current 5-year plan includes starting these old-age-friendly cities initiatives, and by 2020, the Chinese hope to provide 90 percent of care for older people in their homes.

Both in Japan—where a tsunami erased the existing system—and in

China—where there is little installed infrastructure—planners are not burdened by past care models and can think about service delivery anew, along with the business model that will support it, and, finally, the technology needed to make the new models a reality. In contrast, the historic need to defend existing industries that do not want to disappear and that may be reluctant to transform is entrenched in the United States.

FROM MAINFRAME TO PERSONAL HEALTH

In the United States, what business processes and innovation techniques can change the model of care?, Dishman asked. "For a long time, I've been calling this a shift from mainframe to personal health," Dishman said. Many workshop participants described the impetus for such a shift: the demographic imperative. By 2017, Dishman said, "we will have more people on the planet who are over the age of 65 than under age 5 for the first time in human history." Aging populations and rising health care costs are phenomena worldwide. Many countries are "dealing with the triple aim [improving the quality of patient care, improving population health, and reducing the overall cost of care]," he said, even if they do not call it that. They worry about preventing the same costly chronic conditions that they see today in the cohorts that follow. They see the need for elder services outstripping the workforce, producing health care worker shortages and creating immigration challenges around the world.

What they desire is to "shift left," that is, to get more people on the end of the health continuum with lower levels of chronic disease, lower levels of functional impairment, lower costs of health care, and a higher quality of life (see Figure 3-1). Even for people with health problems, care can often be moved left in the diagram in Figure 3-1, he believes, from acute and residential care to home health care.

Innovations in policy or technology may help accomplish the move to the left in the diagram in Figure 3-1. The migration of technologies that help that happen is already occurring, Dishman said, especially in other parts of the world. He suggested that this migration of technologies raises significant questions for the United States, including the following:

- What are the safety and security implications?
- What does this migration mean from a regulatory perspective?
- How can skills be shifted so that people can start performing tasks considered to be the purview of the people on the right of the diagram in Figure 3-1, because there will not be enough capacity on the right?
- How is time shifted to the left in the diagram in Figure 3-1 so that preventive care and fundamental primary care can be done to pre-

vent those bad events that force people to the right of the diagram from ever happening?

Dishman noted that when his Intel team proposes any research or product development or policy work, it is held against this model and assessed for whether it will move care toward the left of the diagram in Figure 3-1 or help keep it on the left. It is not that hospitals and other institutions will disappear, he said, but they will be smaller, and capacity will exist elsewhere in the community. Capacity will be distributed to the home, the workplace, and elsewhere.

The Intel workforce was a test population for this concept, which was tested in three phases. At first, the effort was to encourage employees to sign up for consumer-directed health plans and to start to think differently about their relationship with their health plans. The second phase was the establishment on the Intel campus of Health for Life centers that included primary care and provided employees with risk assessment and follow-up coaching, as desired. Now, the company requires its providers to deliver home-based health care as the default model, to use telehealth and mobile technologies, and to track quality goals for individual employees and the workforce as a whole, which are the basis for payment.

Dishman acknowledged that Intel is learning as it goes along and is still "struggling to figure out this distributed capacity." However, the workplace is a key node of care now and will become larger. He noted that this approach flies in the face of some 230 years of hospital history, which says

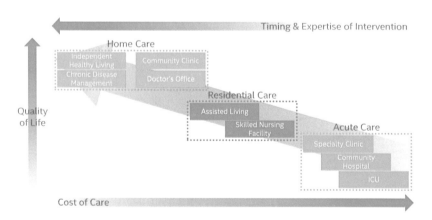

FIGURE 3-1 Intel strategy for innovation: shifts in place, skills, and time from the mainframe model to the personal health model.
NOTE: ICU = intensive care unit.
SOURCE: Reprinted with permission from Eric Dishman, Intel.

that, if you have a medical problem, you "make a pilgrimage to a place where the experts can be with their experts' technology, and you time share that system, just like we used to time share the early computers." Continuing the analogy, he said, "We couldn't conceptualize back then that the power of personal computing was going to be that it would become truly personal. . . . It's yours and you can do with it what you want."

Health care needs to move similarly from a mainframe model to a personal health model, Dishman said. The mainframe model is simply the wrong tool for the job for the vast majority of care, he said. Around the world, Intel social scientists have mapped out people's key nodes of health care, and although they mention their local hospital—for the most part, in a positive way—as their node of care, many other nodes of care exist. Furthermore, the people who are key to their care are not just hospitalists but also therapists, gerontologists, and the librarian who is helping them find information on the Internet. Every person has a different configuration for their "lived reality of health."

In the future, the health care system will not be sustainable, he said, unless it first has an information system, a reward system, and a model of care that takes into account that sort of community-based care, with the home—and probably the workplace—being key nodes. Step one of moving from the mainframe to the personal health approach is distributing the capacity, he said, which depends on skill shifting, place shifting, and time shifting toward the activities that are leftward in the diagram in Figure 3-1.

The second requirement, he said, is for all the separate body parts and systems and for all the cellular-level understandings to be reintegrated into whole-person care. Even though the development of specialty care has been important in providing an understanding of the science behind health and illness, specialists easily become unintentionally biased by the drugs that they study, the problems that they understand, and the treatment approaches that are making their careers successful, he said. Patients who understand that their clinicians may have different backgrounds and motives seek second, third, fourth, and fifth opinions. "You don't know what blinders any individual who is making these life-and-death decisions for you have," he said.

The application of big data analytics to claims data may produce more robust risk assessments at the population level but may not inform the choices of an individual patient, Dishman continued. Consumer-generated data coming from smart phones and health applications can also feed the system to develop a model of care for the individual patient. For example, Intel is working with The Michael J. Fox Foundation for Parkinson's Research to capture consumer-generated data on Parkinson's disease in a search for ways to monitor disease progression more carefully, to titrate medications more accurately, and to differentiate the different kinds of

Parkinson's disease to look for treatment targets. "We have to have an informatics that can personalize care down to that level," he said.

Finally, the inclusion of family members and neighbors as part of the care team requires new kinds of training and creates new kinds of care workers, as is happening in China, he said. Also required are incentives to track the quality of care that neighbors and family members provide. Technology can help with both monitoring and "anticipatory analytics" to assess the likelihood of problems, such as falls or medication lapses, before they happen. At the same time, efforts are needed to shore up social support and social networks. "If you can't maintain the social network, then you have to rely on institutional systems," he said.

PILLARS OF PERSONAL HEALTH

Dishman identified the three pillars of personal health to be care anywhere, care networking, and care customization. The care anywhere concept represents the shift from institutions to mobile, home-based, and community-based care, with the understanding that today home health care can include a much broader range of options and produce care whose quality is much higher than that of traditional notions of home health care, tightly circumscribed as they are by policy, staff training, reimbursement, and client expectations.

Care networking includes the technology infrastructure, business models, and organizational models that allow care to be shifted from solo to team-based practice, along with the information technology systems that connect all these people and devices. Clinical decision support tools today are geared to the information needs of individual clinicians and not to teams of providers and not to trained family members and neighbors. Ideally, everyone in a care network for an individual should receive data updates and information on any changes in the care plan as the patient's goals change or new clinical data or caregiver observations emerge. Dishman said, "Groupware for care decision support will be a key capability going forward."

Care customization manages the shift from population-based to person-based treatment. Although that includes personalization based on genomics, it also means the use of people's smartphones with intelligent algorithms that help them, for example, take their medications on time. Early experiments demonstrated that consistent positive behavior change is possible, as long as clinicians communicate with people in the way in which they prefer. Delivering the support for behavior change is easy to do now; "the hard part is figuring out what works and what does not" in the context of mass customization.

Several shifts of the health care system that would shore up the three pillars are needed, Dishman said, and they can be supported by technology. Some examples include the following:

- Moving from professional care to more self-care. Dishman's group has taught frail seniors to do self-care. These individuals are able to provide self-care if the technologies are usable and the benefits (the value proposition) to them are clear. Even if only 20 percent of patients can take on self-care, it would move the needle on cost, quality, and access, Dishman indicated. That 20 percent of patients would be the classic early adopters, and over time, more people will be able to take on the self-care tasks.
- Moving from transaction-based care to care coordination. Software tools can facilitate such a move by supporting teams, as mentioned above, and providing status reports in real time.
- Moving from "medical-ized" records to "life-ized" ones. Data that are broader than the data that are traditionally of interest to the medical community need to be included in the records for the patient, although whether those data will be included in different data systems or in some way combined into a single system has yet to be determined.
- Moving from stand-alone technologies to integrated ones. Tele-health and remote patient monitoring increasingly will not rely on specific devices but will be embedded into everyday devices. Technical and policy challenges exist, Dishman said, "but that world is coming."

"We have to get out of this mind set that everything we need to do needs to be expensive, purpose built, and started from scratch." Dishman said the future will also leverage technologies already on the diffusion-of-innovation path. They also will become increasingly less expensive and more widely available. An example is the automated external defibrillator, now a not-uncommon piece of consumer electronic equipment. The result is the consumerization of medical devices and the medicalization of consumer devices.

Another trend, he said, will be to enable clinicians to provide care wherever they are: in the clinic, in the hospital, in someone's home, or in a community health center. The tablet computers that they carry will use an infrastructure that gives them access to all the information that they need, although he said that the technology industry will need to develop ways to facilitate the work flow for highly mobile clinicians.

For care customization, the shift to genomics and proteomics is happening rather quickly in cancer and rare inherited disorders, Dishman said, and the computing power needed is also becoming less expensive and more widely available. Predictive modeling will enable more precise and therefore more effective therapies. Analysis of the information obtained by sequencing of a patient's genome and analysis of the parts of the body that control the immune system, metabolism, or any other system that has gone wrong will allow custom drugs to be delivered.

The incorporation of patient goals and care plans into a medical record "is actually a pretty difficult machine-learning problem," Dishman said. Although the creation of a database field called "patient goals" is relatively simple, the analytics that would allow the system to adapt to these goals and suggest ways to achieve them are not. Another data management problem that technology may be able to solve is automation of at least parts of the lengthy documentation tasks that home health care workers are currently required to perform. The time that it takes to complete these tasks subtracts substantially from the time that they have to spend with their clients, or if they hurry the job, the care activities that they perform may not be recorded—or reimbursed.

The results from the first attempt to use any of these systems have not been 100 percent accurate, even though they may have been a vast improvement over those obtained at the baseline, before implementation of the new system, Dishman said. This is another lesson from this work: "Will we wait and say the technology has to be perfect before we can actually use it?" he asked. The better approach will be to iterate over time, and even "the 'good enough' may provide some powerful interventions in quality."

PRINCIPLES FOR THE EVOLUTION OF HEALTH CARE

Rather than a focus on technology, Dishman suggested a set of principles that will facilitate the evolution of health care and the previously described "shift to the left" (see Figure 3-1):

- Shift the place of care to the least restrictive setting.
- Shift skills to patients and caregivers and stop fighting the licensure and protectionism turf wars.
- Shift the time of care so that it is proactive and not reactive.
- Shift payments from individual providers to teams of providers of care and shift payments so that outcomes that reflect the use of a holistic approach are achieved.
- Shift the technology used from specialized equipment to everyday life technologies, but do it within a framework that does not start with technology.

The starting point for these changes, Dishman said, is the social covenant that asserts, "We as a culture have decided this is how we're going to set ourselves up for people who need care and those who provide it." From that, evolve government policy and a framework that includes a financial system. Within that framework is a networked model of care that has a work flow. Within that model of care is embedded the technology. In other words, to use innovation to overcome the demographic dilemma, the social covenant and care models need to be used as the starting point, he said. All the other fundamental decisions about care models, work flows, workforce needs, and optimization of resources for results, followed by determination of sustainable business and payment models, need to come before it is determined what technology infrastructure is needed to support it.

Dishman said that home health care today is "relegated to a niche," to an additional capability to be added to the mainframe model. His challenge to the workshop participants was to think about the workforce and business models that will be needed so that home- and community-based health care can become the default and hospital-based care—according to the mainframe model—becomes the exception.

QUESTIONS AND COMMENTS

An open discussion followed Dishman's presentation. Workshop participants were able to give comments and ask questions. The following section summarizes the discussion session.

Steven Landers, Visiting Nurse Association Health Group, asked about the immediate opportunities to achieve benefits from the expansion of home health care, short of conceptually changing the whole health care system, even, he said, if the kind of evolution toward "care everywhere" is the ultimate goal. Dishman responded that those who provide home health care and long-term services and supports, even though they are sort of a backwater for mainframe care and are often not taken seriously, are the parts of the system that actually understand what needs to happen in the new care model. Dishman said that at Intel he teaches a course on leadership and that one of the principles that he teaches is that great leaders balance between practical thinking and possibility thinking and must be able to do both. He believes that home health care could be one of the disruptive forces that make the rest of the health care industry recognize that whole-person care is needed, especially for older people but also for people of all ages.

Erin Iturriaga, National Institutes of Health, noted that Washington, DC, has 14 villages that are part of the village movement, according to the World Health Organization's age-friendly city model, and that each village is attached to a wellness center. Nationally, she said, the movement is looking for support from cities and states rather than support from the federal government. She asked Dishman if he thought that this model, which sounds similar to what is happening in Japan, could work in the United

States. Dishman responded that by use of the village model, it should be possible to innovate in terms of the care model, the payment model, and the technology used and that if the village model is used long enough this mode of organization will become natural for the people who are involved. He suggested that these villages can become locations for real-life experiments. In general, real-life experiments are hard to come by, he said. Instead, people merely test pieces of a model or test them for too short a period of time and with workers who have to do their old jobs as well as whatever new components that the experiment includes.

Gail Hunt, National Alliance for Caregiving, said that on the previous day of the workshop it became clear that a lot of pressure exists to push more and more of the caregiving tasks off onto the family caregivers, whether or not they are willing or able to handle them. Shifting of skills must require an assessment of the primary caregiver's capacity, Hunt said, as well as that of other family members who would be able to help. Dishman agreed, stating that this is part of his model. The term "family caregiver" can include neighbors and, in some cases, community health workers with various levels of training. Whoever it is, he said, that person is assessed for both their ability and willingness to perform needed tasks, and there are some incentives for them to be assessed. They may be trained in multiple areas—a little home repair, some social work, and clinical care relevant to chronic disease. "I don't know what to call that person," he said. The multiple demands that come into play are part of why the system that assesses quality needs to track the care being provided and make sure that caregivers are not overwhelmed.

Amy Berman, The John A. Hartford Foundation, expressed concern that progress toward supporting good-quality care at home is moving too slowly. In part, she said, this is because not enough geriatric expertise with which to develop the core of these infrastructures or the decision-making support exists and that not enough physicians and nurses are available to care for the older population. Dishman agreed that when no standards are in place, experts from mixed disciplines should be brought in to identify best practices. "One of the things that health care is not good at, almost anywhere in the world, is having a formal and iterative innovation process," he said. In pilot tests, people focus on the wrong problems, they do not learn from past innovations, and they do not have an iterative mind set that, once they have met a baseline set of safety and security standards, says, "We don't have to get it all right in the beginning."

4

Key Issues and Trends

Larger contextual issues (e.g., population health, payment policy) have implications for how home health care may need to change to meet future needs. This chapter describes three presentations that explored overarching trends currently being seen and how they may affect planning for the future role of home health care.

TRENDS IN POPULATION HEALTH

Tricia Neuman
Kaiser Family Foundation

Home Health Care Under Medicare and Medicaid

In home health care, the typical silos of Medicare and Medicaid do occasionally interact and overlap, but they are not truly integrated, affirmed Neuman. Medicare is an entitlement program that covers Americans ages 65 years and older and people under age 65 years with permanent disabilities in a uniform way across the country. Medicaid, by definition, is more complicated because of the combination of federal requirements and the different eligibility and benefit rules of each of the 50 states. The low-income people who are eligible for Medicaid and who receive home health care services often are also covered under Medicare (and are referred to as dually eligible), which is their primary coverage.

Medicaid is frequently thought of as a program for long-term services and supports (LTSS), but home health care is not really that entity, Neuman said. Home-based medical services (including nursing services; home health aides; and medical supplies, appliances, and equipment) are mandatory benefits under Medicaid, but the broader array of home- and community-based services is optional.[1] Even so, states may impose limits on their Medicaid home health care programs. Five states have put limits on program costs, and 25 states and the District of Columbia limit service hours. The benefit is typically covered under fee-for-service arrangements, although many states are moving toward the use of capitation, she said. As in Medicare's home health care program, a physician needs to provide a written plan of care for recipients to be eligible for home health care services.

Mandatory benefits for individuals who qualify for Medicaid home health care include part-time or intermittent visits by a registered nurse; home health aide services provided by credentialed workers employed by participating home health agencies; and appropriate medical equipment, supplies, and appliances. Physical and occupational therapy and speech pathology and audiology services are optional benefits. Fifteen state Medicaid programs allow recipients to arrange their own services, including providing payment to family caregivers. These self-directed services programs have generally proved successful in reducing unmet patient needs and improving health outcomes, quality of life, and recipient satisfaction at a cost comparable to that of traditional home health agency–directed service programs.

In the traditional Medicare program, which uses fee-for-service payments, it has been relatively easy to track how much that public insurance pays for various types of services, including home health care, Neuman said. However, as increasing numbers of Medicare and Medicaid beneficiaries are moving into capitated plans, estimation of the number of people receiving services, how much they are receiving, and what government source is paying for these services becomes harder. Under fee-for-service programs, Medicare currently pays the largest share of home health care expenditures (44 percent), even with its relatively narrow eligibility criteria, followed by Medicaid (38 percent) (see Figure 4-1). Private health insurance and other third-party payers pay about 10 percent, and another 8 percent is paid out-of-pocket. Neuman noted that the amount of out-of-pocket spending is probably understated, because no reliable ways of capturing these data exist.

Home health care remains a relatively small piece of total Medicare and Medicaid spending. As noted above, the Medicaid expenditure may be an underestimate because such a large percentage of Medicaid recipients

---

[1] The broad category of home- and community-based services includes assistance with activities of daily living (ADLs), such as eating, bathing, and dressing; assistance with instrumental activities of daily living (IADLs), such as preparing meals and housecleaning; adult day health care programs; home health aide services; and case management services.

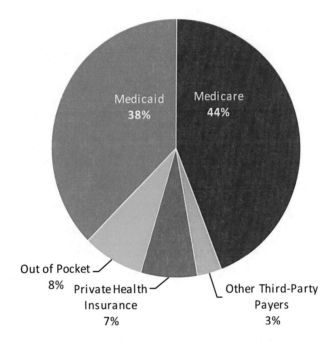

FIGURE 4-1 Total home health care spending, 2012: $78 billion.
NOTE: Estimates of national health care expenditures on home health care also include spending on hospice by home health agencies. Total Medicaid spending includes both state and federal spending. Home health care includes medical care provided in the home by freestanding home health agencies. Medical equipment sales or rentals not billed through home health agencies and nonmedical types of home care (e.g., Meals on Wheels, the services of workers who perform chores, friendly visits, or other custodial services) are excluded.
SOURCE: Kaiser Family Foundation analysis of National Health Expenditure Data, by type of service and source of funds, calendar years 1960 to 2012. Reprinted with permission from Tricia Neuman, Kaiser Family Foundation.

are in managed care plans, which are paid on a per capita and not a per service basis.

Who Is Served?

The utilization of home health care rises with the number of chronic conditions and the functional impairments that people have, Neuman said (see Figure 4-2).

About two-thirds of all Medicare home health care users have four or more chronic conditions or at least one functional impairment. "When

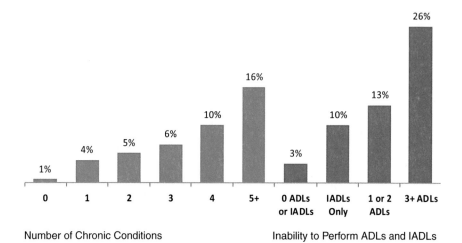

FIGURE 4-2 Percentage of beneficiaries using home health care, by characteristic, 2010.
NOTE: ADLs = activities of daily living; IADLs = instrumental activities of daily living.
SOURCE: Kaiser Family Foundation analysis of Medicare Current Beneficiary Survey, 2010. Reprinted with permission from Tricia Neuman, Kaiser Family Foundation.

you are talking about [people receiving] home health care," Neuman said, "you're talking about a population that is often physically compromised and cognitively compromised. These are people with multiple challenges." Although most of these challenges arise in the context of aging, they also face the population of people with disabilities covered by Medicare.

Neuman presented data indicating that home health care usage overall, the number of home health care visits per user, and Medicare spending per user all rise with age, as does the use of many other health care services, including inpatient care, skilled nursing care, and physician services, and the use of some drugs (but not hospice care). The age–per capita spending curve for each of these services has a peak. For example, Neuman noted that physician services and outpatient drug spending peak at age 83 years, declining thereafter, and that after age 89 years, hospital expenditures start to drop. Spending on home health care does not peak until age 96 years, and spending on skilled nursing facilities peaks at age 98 years.

Although only 9 percent of the traditional (i.e., non-managed care) Medicare population receives home health care services, the health care spending for these individuals accounts for 38 percent of traditional Medicare spending. This is another reflection of their high degree of impairment and need. Neuman posed fundamental questions about these patterns of care, including the following:

- Are beneficiaries receiving care in the most appropriate setting?
- Are they receiving good-quality care in the place where they want to be?
- Does this pattern of care optimally balance federal, state, and family budgets?
- How will the nation finance care for an aging population?

Overall, the use of home health care services has increased in recent years, Neuman said, reflecting both an aging population and the rise in the incidence of chronic conditions noted earlier. However, spending on home health care, which had been rising concomitantly, has leveled off in recent years, even though home health care serves more people. It is not absolutely clear why this is, Neuman said, and then suggested that it may be due in part to payment reductions from the Patient Protection and Affordable Care Act of 2010 (ACA)[2] and greater recent efforts to address fraud in some pockets of the country.

Effects of Policy Changes

Neuman stated that policy changes can spur innovations affecting home health care. These innovations are often aimed at the integration of systems of acute care and LTSS for dually eligible individuals and the development of team-based geriatric care. An example of such innovations, she said, includes the American Academy of Home Care Medicine's Independence at Home initiative.[3]

How well home health care will fit into emerging models of care remains uncertain, Neuman said. Home health care is a relatively small player in these system reforms, and it will take effort to ensure that it can continue to play its important role, she said.

---

[2] Patient Protection and Affordable Care Act of 2010, Public Law 111-148, 111th Cong., 2nd sess. (March 23, 2010).

[3] See http://www.iahnow.com (accessed December 24, 2014).

TRENDS IN PUBLIC POLICY

Douglas Holtz-Eakin
American Action Forum

Holtz-Eakin began his remarks by underscoring the "fundamentally unsustainable health care cost trajectory" that the nation is on, "even with the good news we have had about the pace of health care spending in recent years." Federal budget deficits will grow relative to the gross domestic product, and in a decade, interest payments are projected to be larger than the U.S. Department of Defense budget, producing a tight money environment.

At the center of these difficulties, he said, are the programs that pay 80 percent of the home health care bills: Medicare and Medicaid. Medicare is spending its funds faster than payroll taxes and premiums are replenishing them and will come under increasing financial pressure. Medicaid faces similar pressures, especially at the state level.

The home health care industry's financial condition looks especially precarious, said Holtz-Eakin, with some 40 percent of home health care providers expected to be in debt in just a few years. Moreover, new U.S. Department of Labor rules mandating overtime pay for workers not previously receiving it will boost agency costs, he said, if and when they go into effect. In the home, LTSS have been provided by family members, but in the future, this source of care will be less available, because family members will be working.

Despite this combination of pressures, opportunities also exist, Holtz-Eakin said. Keeping frail elders with chronic diseases and disabilities out of acute care could save a lot of money, so "the opportunity at the front end to really solve the Medicare cost problem is a serious one." Research also suggests that home health care can play a substantial cost-saving role in post-acute care as well. To take advantage of such opportunities, the home health care sector will be required to document not just their cost savings but also the quality of the care that they provide. The combination of lower cost and high quality creates a value proposition for policy makers and taxpayers, Holtz-Eakin said. Further, the traditional dichotomy between health care services and LTSS needs to end, he believes.

Holtz-Eakin said that policy makers are "trying to fix these programs at the margins," when what is needed is "a fundamental rethinking of how we deliver all these services." Further, he believes, the voters will want to go with comfortable proposals, and "I'm not sure that will be enough to get this right going forward."

Although technological advances have helped resolve a large number of major policy problems, in this situation, it is not clear what such an advance would be, he said. For example, what agency will approve new health technology devices? Are health care applications going to be regulated by the U.S. Food and Drug Administration (FDA) or by the Federal Communications Commission? When a service crosses state lines (as with telehealth), difficulties with state-based licensing and scope of practice regulations may arise.

TRENDS IN THE REAL WORLD

Barbara A. McCann
Interim HealthCare

Several trends help describe the reality of U.S. home health care, as McCann sees it from her perspective as a medical social worker.

Limitations in the Design of the Medicare Home Health Care Benefit for Today's Population

Most people are unaware of home health care services until a moment of crisis, when a staff member from the hospital, inpatient rehabilitation center, or nursing home advises them that their loved one is being discharged and arrangements for care in the home need to be made, McCann said. Thousands of Medicare beneficiaries who are older or have disabilities and their families have had to face this crisis and are receiving home health care, but the benefit is a poor fit to their needs, McCann said. Designed almost 50 years ago, the home health care benefit emphasizes recovery from acute illness and the opportunity for health improvement, and it presumes that the beneficiary's health problems will end. It does not emphasize wellness or prevention, and it does not pay for comfort care or palliation at the end of life.

Patients receiving Medicare home health care services must be homebound, and once they are no longer confined to home, the benefit ends. However, "chronic disease goes on, [and] medications continue to come into the house," McCann said. At that point, home health care providers have no one to hand the patient over to or transition to for ongoing care and coordination. Patient-centered medical homes solve this problem, she said, but they are far from universal.

Managing Continuous Transitions

Despite these challenges, home health care is being reinvented to serve as an important piece in the continuum of chronic care. In accountable care organizations, with their capitated structure, some providers are working around the strictures of the Medicare home health care benefit and ensuring that patients receive the needed services. Transitions not only between care settings—especially hospital to home—but also during the period of time after a physician's visit are times when patients definitely need help, even with an issue as basic as communication. "They can't remember what they talked about or who they told about which symptom," McCann said, "and they certainly can't remember what the doctor told them to do or what medications to take."

McCann noted that the home health care nurse can sit with the patient and family member or other caregiver and review medications, dosage schedules, and other medical instructions to help the family become organized about the patient's health care needs. "The reality of health [care] in the home is the reality of the kitchen table. That's where health decisions are made, and that's where health is managed," she said. Later in the workshop, Thomas E. Edes, U.S. Department of Veterans Affairs, agreed with this characterization, saying "the gold standard of medication reconciliation happens at the kitchen table."

The most typical problems, McCann said, are

- Remembering to take medications,
- Knowing what the symptoms of problems are and when and from whom to seek help,
- Verifying that the individual or family member(s) makes an appointment with the community physician within 1 to 2 weeks post-discharge and that the individual has transportation,
- Making sure that reliable arrangements for meal preparation are in place, and
- Checking the patient's ability to perform ADLs safely or whether arrangements are needed to make these activities easier or safer so that the individual can stay at home.

Finally, as a social worker, McCann emphasized the need for socialization by asking, "How [do] we keep people engaged daily?" Taking care of all of these important dimensions of care will be important to each patient and family well past the 30 or 60 days of Medicare's home health care benefit or a post-acute care service.

Data Shortfalls

McCann said that many health care data exist but that almost no information on home health care is available. Since 2000, whenever a Medicare or a Medicaid patient has received skilled care, nursing services, or therapy at home, providers have had to collect more than 100 pieces of data about that patient and service. This requirement holds whether the patient is covered by traditional fee-for-service Medicare, Medicare Advantage, Medicaid skilled care, or Medicaid managed care. "We have data on millions of episodes of care sitting in a database somewhere that have not been analyzed," she said.

Although home health care providers receive some performance information, they do not know what combination of service timing, staff specialty, or coverage type results in better (or worse) patient outcomes. Nor do the available data reflect what additional personal care and support services not paid for by Medicare and Medicaid that the patient has obtained privately. It may be that these services make crucial differences to patient well-being.

New Program Models

McCann has encountered a number of hurdles to collaborative work in home health care that need to be overcome. For example, physicians assess pain differently than do physical therapists, and physical therapists assess pain differently than do home health agency personnel, she said. Nor do these three groups assess dependence in ADLs in the same way, making it more difficult to assess change or improvement. Furthermore, little common language for the establishment of outcome measures exists, she said.

Collaboration is likewise a feature of the demonstration programs for dually eligible individuals, she noted, in which the goal is better programmatic coordination throughout the continuum of care. This is to be accomplished through the integration and alignment of federal Medicare and state Medicaid funds into a single source of financial support for social as well as medical needs.

Home health care does not mean that a person is always in the home, McCann said. It may mean having a smartphone application that reminds a person to take medication;[4] it may be the availability of a nurse or pharmacist via email or the telephone. Responsive cognitively appropriate and age-appropriate communication systems would help avoid unnecessary 911 calls.

This work involves more than managing illness; it means taking a wellness, preventive, and habilitation approach. She said, "I may not be able to [offer full rehabilitation to you], but I can help you live better in your home." McCann concluded, "This is what we have to remember about the beauty of home care: it's at home."

---

[4] A participant noted that FDA has a guidance on mobile applications.

QUESTIONS AND COMMENTS

An open discussion followed the panelists' presentations. Workshop participants were able to give comments and ask questions of the panelists. The following sections summarize the discussion session.

Definitions

Mary Brady, FDA, said that a standard definition of home health care is needed. The definition used by FDA's Center for Devices and Radiological Health includes concepts of wellness and the usefulness of devices not only in the home but also at school, during transport, or wherever a person is and includes whatever devices are needed to keep healthy those who are living well outside of a clinical facility, she said.

Families

Amy Berman, The John A. Hartford Foundation, asked how home health care should respond to the declining numbers and availability of family caregivers. In current policy, she said, these individuals are not part of the unit of care. Innovations to address that problem have not worked well, said Holtz-Eakin, but "the key to solving it is to get away from the silos" and to provide a broader range of services. Neuman emphasized that the data on the performance of some innovative models may not be available for a number of years. She said, "We need to get more evidence about how well those systems are working for seriously impaired people before we think that managed care and capitation will be a solution for care, even though they may be clearly a solution for budgets."

One workshop participant commented that home health care needs to address not only cognitive and physical impairments but also the emotional needs of patients dealing with a new diagnosis and family members dealing with the exigencies of patient care.

Chris Herman, National Association of Social Workers, commented that difficult transitions do not end for families when hospice or home health care services appear. They reemerge each time that a new practitioner in that program goes into the patient's home. Practitioners must continue to weave those programmatic connections together and help people understand them, she said. Neuman agreed, stating that the issue of transitions also needs to be thought about outside the hospital-to-home context. People in retirement communities, assisted living facilities, and other settings may not have family nearby for the kitchen-table conversations that McCann described.

Cynthia Boyd, Johns Hopkins University, asked about what is being done to improve communication among patients and caregivers at home, home health care providers, and the rest of the health care system. McCann reiterated the importance of making sure that patients and their families understand their situation, what can be done about it, and whom to call. This information can be conveyed in multiple languages, through the use of drawings, or in other imaginative forms of communication so that individuals and families understand what is happening and what options they have. However, what is often needed, she said, is to have someone available to answer questions at the moment that they arise. Call centers that are linked to pharmacies can help individuals get answers to questions about medications. Sometimes, just having a live person to talk to can reduce a person's anxiety. Communication of patient and family concerns back to other parts of the health care system is relatively easy in some of the more progressive patient-centered medical homes but is not so easy in other care environments. Said McCann, it should be explicit "who is responsible for those transitions and staying coordinated across time."

Jimmo v. Sebelius

Herman also asked about the anticipated impact of the *Jimmo v. Sebelius* case[5] and the resultant changes to Medicare for beneficiaries. Workshop participant Judith Stein, Center for Medicare Advocacy and a lead counsel in the case, responded. The case was brought on behalf of Ms. Jimmo and others as a national class action, she said, to address a long-standing problem that Medicare coverage is regularly denied on the basis of beneficiaries' restoration potential and not on the basis of whether they require skilled care. For many people with long-term and chronic conditions, the likelihood of health restoration may be negligible, yet skilled care may well be required for them to maintain their condition or to prevent or slow its worsening. Stein said that the *Jimmo* case should help people receive the benefits that they are entitled to under the Medicare law and that will allow them to stay at home.

Cost of Care

Several workshop participants raised the issue of cost throughout the workshop. Namely, is home health care less expensive than the equivalent

---

[5] "On January 24, 2013, the U.S. District Court for the District of Vermont approved a settlement agreement in the case of *Jimmo v. Sebelius*, in which the plaintiffs alleged that Medicare contractors were inappropriately applying an 'improvement standard' in making claims determinations for Medicare coverage involving skilled care (e.g., the skilled nursing facility, home health, and outpatient therapy benefits)" (CMS, 2014).

care in a nursing home setting? Neuman responded that no good studies of this question have been conducted. The provision of comprehensive services full-time in the home would be more expensive than the provision of those services in a nursing home. Holtz-Eakin said that the focus should be on value and not just cost. What is needed, he said, is acquisition and analysis of the data on home health care to identify quality outcomes and best practices. As an illustration, Andrea Brassard, American Nurses Association, noted that her research on intensive home health care services in New York City in the 1990s found that these services did delay nursing home admissions and mortality among the sickest population. Holtz-Eakin noted that many studies have documented successful provider experiences and cost-saving business models with particular patient populations. However, to be suitable for adoption as part of the Medicare benefit, a study's positive findings need to be generalizable to the population as a whole, he said, because "Medicare is for everybody."

According to Brassard, the requirement that a physician sign off on orders for home health care or have a face-to-face encounter with the patient is inefficient and creates delays in dealing with patients' problems. In most instances, she said, a nurse practitioner (NP), clinical nurse specialist, or physician assistant should be able to do this certification. Although the U.S. Congress has been concerned that allowing other health care professionals to certify that a patient requires home health care would increase costs by increasing the demand for home health care, the current inefficiencies are also costly, she said. Brassard asserted that the problem will become more acute in 25 to 30 years, when predictions indicate that one in every three primary care providers will be an NP; today that number is one in five. The Congressional Budget Office (CBO), which determines the cost of proposed legislation, has difficulty with projections that are long term, given that congressional policy making is mostly short term. Moreover, said Holtz-Eakin, CBO measures only costs, and if proposed legislation has nonmonetary benefits, organizations need "to get policy makers to advocate on behalf of those benefits."

Erin Iturriaga, National Institutes of Health, raised the issue of the growing population of aging individuals in prisons. To save money, she said, states are releasing older long-stay prisoners early, shifting the costs of their care from the prison system to other payers, including Medicaid. Data on inmate health are not part of typical health care databases, and states have no way of budgeting for this influx.

Combining Medical Care and Social Needs

Michael Johnson, BAYADA Home Health Care, noted that different definitions of home health care seem to be constricted by the requirements of the programs that are paying for it. A broader conceptualization of home- and community-based services may be needed. He asked how the Medicare focus on disease and drugs can be rebalanced with considerations about prevention and pre-acute care or about improving function, nutrition, and maybe even cognition. Holtz-Eakin responded that the current programs, as they exist, are not built for the future. The country's approach is ad hoc, he said, and was invented through regulation and minor policy changes. Although it makes sense to take outcomes, including functional outcomes, as the focus, the Medicare program was designed almost five decades ago to serve people with acute-care stays and is now being asked to serve a population whose biggest problems are chronic diseases. The recent Senate Commission on Long-Term Care[6] concluded that although significant program changes are needed, to provide more LTSS, there is no clear way to pay for them, Neuman said. She agreed that working with people early (providing pre-acute care instead of only post-acute care) to prevent functional decline would be an important strategy. Which provider will do this is uncertain: "There are a lot of people competing for that space," she said. The mind set that long-term care is nursing home care must change, said McCann. Today, long-term care is simply the reality of chronic disease, aging, and disability. The evaluation of models from other countries—especially Australia—may help change that perception.

Bruce Leff, Johns Hopkins University School of Medicine, asked if the breakdown of silos among programs will emerge from new business models, including a greater penetration of managed care, or if it will require another big political battle. Holtz-Eakin predicted that both are likely but that change can certainly build on some of the essential organizational innovations currently under way. Regardless of the delivery model, however, payment should be made on the basis of patient outcomes. Meanwhile, it should be possible to build on Medicare Advantage and expand what it covers to include not just traditional health care services but also a continuum of health and social supports.

Terrence O'Malley, Massachusetts General Hospital, asked if realigning health care payments through accountable care and managed care organizations is increasing awareness of the importance of social factors in health. That does not seem to be happening as quickly as anticipated, he said. The panelists counseled patience, because promising new models are still only promising and it is too soon to pick winners. If these new models are allowed to run a while, the ones that are successful in reducing costs and improving quality will be revealed, Holtz-Eakin said. The ACA was just the beginning of a health care reform process that will continue for many years. What this workshop is about, he said, is getting home health care right in the end.

---

[6] See http://ltccommission.org (accessed December 24, 2014).

5

The Home Health Care Workforce

Many different people make up the home health care workforce, including professionals (e.g., nurses, physical therapists, physicians) and direct care workers (e.g., home health aides, personal care aides), along with individuals and their families. As in health care in general, home health care depends on a team of individuals working together. In one panel of the workshop, four speakers addressed the role of each person on the home health care team (as well as the team itself) and how to facilitate their roles in ways in which they will be needed for the future ideal state of home health care.

THE VALUE OF TEAM-BASED CARE

Thomas E. Edes
U.S. Department of Veterans Affairs

In the U.S. Department of Veterans Affairs (VA), the home-based primary care program uses a team approach in its pursuit of the triple aim: improving the patient experience of care (quality and satisfaction), improving population health, and reducing per capita care costs. Edes began with the story of one particular veteran, which is presented in Box 5-1.

Home-Based Primary Care in the VA

In the VA, Edes said, home-based primary care is comprehensive, longitudinal primary care delivered in the homes of veterans with serious

BOX 5-1
A Veteran's Story

Edes related the story of a 74-year-old veteran with advanced Parkinson's disease who was struggling to manage at home. Not surprisingly, Edes said, he was developing significant depression. He had been falling a lot. He had lost 40 pounds and had aspiration problems, dementia, and hallucinations. He was treated with deep brain stimulation, but that had not helped him much. He still had serious problems with his gait, muscle spasms, and tremors; and he had difficulty swallowing.

After several hospitalizations, the medical team recommended transition to a nursing home, but the veteran refused, saying, "I'm going to die if I'm admitted to a nursing home." The health care team took his preferences to heart and rewrote the care plan. Instead of the nursing home, he was discharged to home with home-based primary care and home health aide services. Even if it did not change his prognosis, home was where he wanted to be.

The U.S. Department of Veterans Affairs (VA) home-based primary care team worked with his caregivers so that they understood his daily care and support needs. The social worker helped him identify a caregiver for support and socialization through the Veteran Directed Care program (which the VA has in more than half of the states) and connections with the community and identified sources of support for his daily care needs. The rehabilitation therapist provided the help necessary for the veteran to increase the amount of exercise that he received and prevent falls.

In addition, the nurse helped explain a complicated medication management regimen and trained caregivers in the Heimlich maneuver if aspirations occurred. The dietitian worked on improving the patient's nutrition to help him gain weight and taught techniques in preparing foods to avoid triggering esophageal spasms. Meanwhile, the psychologist tackled the problems of isolation and depression. In short, the full team continuously worked to find solutions, including ways to address new problems that arose.

As a result of these comprehensive, integrated efforts, after a year in the program, the veteran displayed a remarkable improvement in health status: he had about half the rate of falls as in the year before enrollment (9 versus 16) and only one hospitalization (versus 5 the previous year), and his weight stabilized. On the psychosocial side, he was less isolated and more involved with his community, which he said improved his quality of life.

Equally important, he felt that he had recovered some of the control over his life that his disease had eroded, and his goals were met: no nursing home, no feeding tube, fewer hospitalizations, and greater activity and community engagement.

SOURCE: As presented by Thomas E. Edes on September 30, 2014.

multiple chronic diseases and disabling conditions who are too sick to go to the clinic. Care is provided by an interdisciplinary team that comprises a nurse, a physician, a social worker, a rehabilitation therapist, a dietitian, a pharmacist, and a psychologist. Since 2006, those teams have included a mental health professional, because "if we do not effectively manage our patients' mental health conditions, we will not effectively manage their medical conditions," Edes said.

This is, admittedly, an expensive team, but, Edes said, "We cannot afford not to have that expensive team." He then described the population that these teams care for: men in advanced stages of disease (a 24 percent annual mortality) with, on average, more than eight chronic medical conditions. About half are dependent in two or more activities of daily living (ADLs), just under half are married, and 30 percent live alone. For those with a caregiver, 30 percent of the caregivers have activity limitations as well, he said. With respect to diagnosis, half of the patients have diabetes, one-third have cancer, 40 percent have depression, about one-third have dementia, 20 percent have schizophrenia, and 20 percent have posttraumatic stress disorder. Although home-based care from the interdisciplinary team is available to veterans regardless of age, most in the program are older, and the proportion of the veteran population age 85 years and older is growing, as it is for all Americans, but it is growing at a much faster rate for the veteran population.

Even though the veterans in this population have high mortality rates, on average, they receive home-based primary care for more than 300 days. To make this program affordable, Edes said, it must focus tightly on the veterans who are in the 5 percent who account for half of the VA's health care costs and not on the 50 percent who account for only 4 percent of costs. "Almost anything you do in that latter population will raise costs," he said.

The goal of the program is to support veterans so that they may remain at home for as long as is feasible with optimal health, safety, independence, and purpose—and at lower cost. Achievement of that goal, Edes said, depends on

- Increases in veterans' access to home-based services,
- Minimization of avoidable hospital days, and
- Prevention or optimization of nursing home care.

Differences from Medicare

Edes drew a distinction between the VA home-based primary care and traditional Medicare home care. The two organizations have different target populations, different processes, and different outcomes. The VA's program provides longitudinal, comprehensive, interdisciplinary care to

TABLE 5-1 Comparison of the VA Home-Based Primary Care and
Medicare Home Health Care

VA Home-Based Primary Care	Medicare Home Health Care
Targets complex chronic disease	Targets remediable conditions
Provides comprehensive primary care	Provides specific problem-focused care
Does not require skilled care	Requires skilled care
Does not require the patient to be homebound	Requires the patient to be homebound
Accepts declining status	Requires improvement
Uses an interdisciplinary team	Uses professionals from one discipline or a multidisciplinary team
Provides longitudinal care	Provides episodic, post-acute care
Reduces hospital days	Has no definitive impact
Has a limited geography and intensity	Is performed anywhere, anytime

SOURCE: Adapted from Beales and Eades, 2009, with permission from Elsevier and Thomas
Edes.

veterans with complex chronic diseases and complements Medicare home
care, which has more limited purposes, as shown in Table 5-1.

Edes noted that the VA program covers key gaps in Medicare home
care that had been emphasized by previous speakers, including the inclusion
of people with complex, multiple chronic conditions and not merely those
with post-acute care needs or remediable conditions; it takes a more comprehensive approach to the provision of care; and it has a focus on patient
needs and not homebound status. Edes said that the care team members
are truly interdisciplinary and work together to create a unified plan of
care for each patient. Moreover, they recognize that they are likely to be
the patient's care provider for the remainder of his life. These advantages
have helped the VA program reduce the numbers of hospital days and total
costs for this high-acuity population.

Where the Medicare home care program is especially helpful to veterans, he said, is in providing post-acute care, providing care on a high-
frequency basis (albeit for a short time), and providing care outside the
geographic reach of the VA home care programs.

Program Outcomes

In 2002, Edes said, the VA analyzed the impact of home-based primary
care involving more than 11,000 veterans before and after implementation

of the primary care program (Beales and Edes, 2009). The researchers found that program participants had 62 percent fewer hospital days and 29 percent fewer admissions, 88 percent fewer nursing home days, and a 21 percent reduction in the 30-day hospital readmission rate. Furthermore, the net cost to the VA was 24 percent lower when the home-based primary care program was implemented, after the cost of the program was accounted for. Currently, some 34,000 veterans receive these services, and enrollment continues to grow. Furthermore, 38 percent of these veterans live in rural areas. Pilot tests are being conducted with the Indian Health Service to expand the program's reach into American Indian populations. Additional analysis has shown that the VA's cost reductions have not been achieved by shifting costs to Medicare. In fact, Edes said, veterans' enrollment in home-based primary care achieved a 25 percent reduction in combined VA and Medicare hospital admissions and a greater reduction—36 percent—in combined hospital days. The result was a 13 percent reduction in combined Medicare and VA (net) costs.

Edes said that results like these meant that the model was included as part of the Patient Protection and Affordable Care Act of 2010 (ACA)[1] as the Independence at Home demonstration program, along with a financing structure to support it. Like the VA home-based primary care program, the Independence at Home model targets complex, chronic, and disabling conditions; provides interdisciplinary, longitudinal care in the home; emphasizes skills in geriatrics care; uses electronic health records; and uses evaluation metrics that include quality and satisfaction, as well as reductions in the number of inpatient days. At a minimum, Independence at Home demonstration sites are projected to produce a 5 percent cost savings, and if they achieve more, the additional savings will be shared with the site. The demonstration is in its third and final year and is operating in 14 single-practice sites and in three consortium projects.

Recently, Edes noted, results from a large 5-year, propensity-matched, case-control study of a similar model involving about 700 intervention patients and three times as many controls were reported (De Jonge et al., 2014). This program provides services to mostly frail elders in the Washington, DC, area using an interdisciplinary team. Edes said that it produced a 17 percent reduction in the total cost of care for the patients receiving the intervention. Some components of care—home health and hospice—were more costly for the intervention group, but these costs were more than offset by the lower costs associated with the reduction in receipt of care in hospitals and skilled nursing facilities and fewer subspecialist visits. Again, he said, the conclusion is that home-based primary care does

---

[1] Patient Protection and Affordable Care Act of 2010, Public Law 111-148, 111th Cong., 2nd sess. (March 23, 2010).

reduce the cost of care for carefully selected individuals but does so only for those who are the most frail. Edes estimates that the Independence at Home model, if it were expanded nationwide, could save the Centers for Medicare & Medicaid Services more than $6 billion per year.

Researchers face methodological challenges in studying these new models. Edes said, "Robust methods of analysis are needed in addition to randomized controlled trials to meet the challenges of evaluating complex interventions involving diverse populations with variable comorbidities receiving individualized care in a rapidly evolving healthcare system" (Edes et al., 2014, p. 1955). The complexity of the patients, the services, and the new organizational structures exceed the ability of randomized controlled trials to trace the effects of these programs.

In an analysis of costs, the Congressional Budget Office found that Medicare costs per beneficiary rose 29 percent between 2000 and 2005, but in the VA, per patient costs rose only 2 percent. This difference, Edes said, is largely attributable to the VA's development of programs specifically for people with serious, complex comorbidities. During those same years, the cost of home hospice services paid for by the VA increased more than 400 percent, the number of inpatient palliative care consults grew 25-fold, the amount of home-based primary care that it provided increased 55 percent, its medical foster home placements nearly tripled, and its home- and community-based services increased 87 percent. Still, overall costs rose only 2 percent.

In 2013, more veterans died in VA hospice inpatient units than in intensive care or other hospital units combined, Edes said. Among those enrolled in home-based primary care and in medical foster homes, about two-thirds die at home. Finally, the overall number of veterans in long-term care increased about 30 percent between 2000 and 2010 because of the sharp rise in the number of veterans aged 85 years and older.

Medical Foster Homes

Edes spoke briefly about the Medical Foster Home program, another long-term care alternative of the VA with costs about half those of nursing home care. This program merges the adult foster home concept with an interdisciplinary team providing home-based primary care. In this case, the foster care provider is taught how to care for the specific patient, and the VA makes any necessary modifications to the home. These foster care providers commit to providing care for the remainder of an older veteran's life and for 3 years for younger veterans, after which the commitment is renewable.

Centrality of Teams

For the 5 percent of the VA patients who account for half of the system's health care costs, teams are essential, Edes said, and perform the following roles:

- Provide personal and caregiver support services;
- Provide comprehensive, interdisciplinary, and longitudinal clinical and home care;
- Provide palliative care in all settings;
- Ensure the optimal use of and alternatives to hospital and nursing home care;
- Introduce appropriate assistive technology in all settings; and
- Ensure that transitional care is integrated into all settings; this integration moves beyond care coordination to the actual presence of members of the team in the home and community, and the establishment of relationships with staff, patients, family caregivers, and other community partners.

When teams have such a central role, they can increase access to care, improve its quality, and reduce its costs, Edes believes, because so much waste is inherent in mismanaged transitions.

In addition to the use of teams, the management of transitions, and integration, technology is another key to improving home care, he said. The VA already has a robust electronic medical records system (the VISTA system), but it may not be accessible in the home or in geographic areas where Internet service is unreliable. For the present, the VA has developed a software package that includes 1 year's worth of a patient's medical records on a laptop. The importance of mobile electronic documentation will increase as point-of-care diagnostics and hospital-at-home programs become more prevalent, he said.

Edes concluded that too many people see the growing population of people with multiple chronic disabling diseases and their concomitant need for long-term services and supports (LTSS) as the problem and the source of the unsustainable rise in health care costs in the United States. However, he said, a refocus on the kinds of services that best serve the small number of people who incur most of the health care costs can both reduce costs and greatly improve the quality of care.

SUPPORTING FAMILIES

Gail Hunt
National Alliance for Caregiving

Hunt began her remarks by emphasizing one of the themes of earlier presentations, which is the importance of the patient–caregiver dyad and how it is at the center of a set of relationships that includes home health care providers, physicians, nurses, therapists, and all the other health care providers. Families and other caregivers play a major role in implementing a patient's care plan—diet, exercise, medication, and so on. For that reason, she said, "we need to think of the family caregiver as a member of the care team" and to build scalable models of care that are truly patient and family centered and that can accommodate people with multiple chronic conditions. Lessons on ways in which to do that may come from states that have created strong home- and community-based care programs that involve not just medical and health care professionals but also individuals who provide supporting services, such as personal care, companionship for people with Alzheimer's disease, and transportation. "If they can't get to the doctor's appointment, the whole system kind of falls apart," she said.

Skilled providers of home care play an important role in training family caregivers, Hunt said. They can also assess both the ability and the willingness of caregivers to meet the demands being placed on them. Some needed services may be too physically or emotionally difficult for a family caregiver to perform (e.g., ostomy care), and the caregiver may require aid from an external source.

Technology—for example, medication reminders, pill dispensers, and passive monitoring systems—can help not only the patient but also the family caregivers, Hunt said, by helping the caregivers manage their time or providing them with efficient ways to connect to the care system. Such aids must be affordable, as they are likely to be paid for out-of-pocket. The developers of technologies need to work with caregivers to design useful, affordable new tools, Hunt suggested.

Hunt identified barriers to the vision of improving caregiver support. These included a lack of data on the return on caregiver investment; the generalizability of existing models; and current Medicare restrictions, such as the requirement that a patient be homebound or a lack of reimbursement for telemedicine in urban areas. Other countries (e.g., Australia) have in place systems for providing long-term assistance to family caregivers, she said. She added that the United Kingdom has also overcome some of the barriers, even for parents of children with disabilities who face a lifelong caregiving responsibility.

Finally, she said, patient goals and patient-reported outcomes are essential in assessing the quality of care. "It is not so much what we did for the patient as what did the patient want and what did the family want?"

DIRECT CARE WORKERS

Robyn I. Stone
LeadingAge

Next to the family, people in the direct care workforce are probably the most important component of the home care system, Stone said. In thinking about whether the problems being discussed at the workshop should be defined as home health care, home care, home- and community-based services, or personal care, she decided to talk about all of these, because direct care workers are present in all of these permutations of the care-at-home sector.

Even though many programs may fit under the broadest rubric of home care, Stone believes that it is important not to use these terms synonymously. It is not just a matter of semantics, she said, but confusion shows up in the data about home care and becomes ever greater in discussions of new service delivery models. Data are collected for at least three categories of direct care providers: home health aides, home care aides or personal care attendants, and hospice aides. Within those are further subcategories. Housekeeping and companion services may or may not be considered in-home care.

Types of Direct Service Workers

The two categories of workers who provide most of the hands-on functional assistance for patients are home care aides and personal care attendants, Stone said. They assist with basic ADLs and personal care (see Chapter 2 for a description of ADLs); they may also assist with instrumental activities of daily living (IADLs).[2] In some situations, they may also be trained to manage medications. They are the workers who have one-on-one relationships with patients, they serve as liaisons with family caregivers, and they provide emotional support. More importantly, "direct service workers are really the eyes and ears of the care system," Stone said. They perform this key observation role in conjunction with family members and when no family member is present. In the next 25 years, because of increased childlessness and the divorce rate in the United States, the number of family caregivers will decrease, Stone indicated. Although relationships between

---

[2] IADLs are complex skills that a person needs to live independently, such as shopping, preparing meals, using the telephone, taking medications, and managing money.

family caregivers and direct care workers are often good, they also can be "really terrible," she said, "with a lot of tension between the two."

Although the number of direct care workers is expected to grow 48 percent between 2010 and 2020, Stone said, these two key occupational categories (home care aides and personal care attendants) are expected to grow 70 percent, and after that, as more Americans reach age 85 years, the demand will likely grow even faster. Wages in this sector are low and have been stagnant for the past decade, she said. Benefits vary widely, and a high proportion of direct care workers are employed only part-time, which further impedes access to benefits. Enforcement of a U.S. Department of Labor plan to extend minimum-wage and overtime protection to home care workers has been delayed as a result of states' concerns about the potential impact on Medicaid programs and industry concerns that families could not afford the increased cost.

"When we think about what we pay them, we wonder how we can get anybody to do this work," she said. Nationally, the people who do take it up are mostly non-Hispanic, middle-aged women. About half are white, and about 35 percent are black, although Stone predicts more diversity in this workforce in coming years, along with the greater diversity in the population of elderly individuals.

The work situation of hospice aides is somewhat better than that of home care or home health care aides, Stone said, as they receive higher wages and have greater access to employer-sponsored health insurance and other employee benefits. Hospice aides are also more likely to be employed full-time and to stay in their jobs. Hospices' more generous wages and employment benefits—as well as the somewhat better training—may result from the higher reimbursement rate for hospice services. "We need to be thinking about bringing the rest of the direct care workforce up at least to where the hospice workers are now," Stone said.

Training Requirements

For Medicare- and Medicaid-certified providers, home aides and hospice aides must have 75 hours of training and pass a competency exam. No federal training requirements exist for home care and personal care aides, and the amount of training varies by state, with many states having no requirements whatsoever. Stone said that a lack of training also may hamper consumer-directed services, such as cash and counseling.[3] Training for the

---

[3] Cash and counseling is "an approach to long-term personal assistance services in which the government gives people cash allowances to pay for the services and goods they feel would best meet their personal care needs and counseling about managing their services" (RWJF, 2013). Under cash and counseling programs, individuals determine who will be paid for provision of personal care services (including family members) and how those services will be provided.

eyes and ears function is especially important, Stone stated, since research has shown that home health aides observe a change in a patient's condition 5 days before a nurse does.

Recruitment and Retention

Problems of low pay and a lack of training suggest to employers and families a lack of competence among direct care personnel, Stone said, rather than a shortage of workers, per se. When the local economy is poor, recruitment is not a problem. Stone's organization, LeadingAge, includes in its membership about 6,000 nonprofit agencies that provide services to the aging population, from nursing homes to assisted living facilities, home health agencies, continuing care retirement communities, low-income housing developments, and many others. When the economy begins to improve, employee turnover among the members begins to rise, she said.

High turnover rates lead to a lack of consistency in care and a succession of individuals providing care in the home, which can negatively affect both the physical and mental well-being of the recipients of care, Stone said. High turnover rates are also hard on an agency's remaining employees, because when the agency is shorthanded, workloads increase. They can potentially affect both the quality of care and the quality of life, she said. Turnover also increases costs for employers and the health care system as a whole. With the cost of replacing a home care worker averaging $4,500 and turnover rates of between 60 and 75 percent, the total costs are enormous.

Stone said that other factors affecting workforce recruitment and retention are the stereotyping of the industry (which is especially true for nursing homes) and working conditions. Home care work can be isolating, with workers having no real sense of community with the other members of an agency's workforce. This area has not been well researched, Stone said.

Improving the Direct Care Workforce

According to Stone, principal strategies to resolve problems with the direct care workforce for home-based care include the following:

- Competency-based training that includes good clinical placements;
- Improved supervision focused on coaching and mentoring;
- Protocols for resolution of problems;
- Continued staff development and career advancement potential, but not necessarily career ladders ("Not every home care aide or personal care attendant wants to be a nurse," Stone said.);
- Policies that permit direct care workers to specialize in, for example, dementia care or medication management;

- Procedures that allow frontline workers to be engaged as part of the care team;
- Improved wages and benefits;
- Training around the challenges of caring for people who have multiple comorbidities and who take multiple medications;
- Training in signals and symptoms of functional decline, depression, social isolation, and the impact of dementia; and
- Training in managing family dynamics and cultural competence.

As an exemplary program, Stone cited the Personal and Home Care Aide State Training (PHCAST) Program, a six-state demonstration program funded through the ACA.[4] North Carolina's PHCAST project, for example, is a four-phase program that develops career lattices and career ladders, is involved with the state's high schools and community colleges, and has established certifications for different levels of training. She also cited the Eldercare Workforce Alliance's advanced direct care worker concept, which, again, proposes career lattices so that workers can become home care and personal care aides with more advanced capabilities. Finally, she noted the Service Employees International Union Healthcare NW Training Partnership, a competency-based apprenticeship program in Washington State involving a school and labor management partnership intended to deliver training to the state's 43,000 home care aides.[5]

Meeting Future Needs

In the long term, Stone predicted, the emerging gap between the need for home care and the available workforce will grow because of a declining availability of individuals able to provide informal care, a decline in the availability of people in the age groups who want to hold these types of jobs, and an increase in demand for home care services brought on by an aging population and shifts of care from institutional settings to the home and community. Although technology—robots, for example—may fill part of the need at some point, for the foreseeable future, "a significant human capital need" will remain, Stone said, although technologies may complement that need.

Also important is the development of new worker pipelines, as the North Carolina PHCAST project did with high school students. Older workers, the unemployed, new immigrants, and former family caregivers may provide new worker pools. The new long-term service delivery models

---

[4] See http://bhpr.hrsa.gov/nursing/grants/phcast.html (accessed December 5, 2014).

[5] See http://www.myseiubenefits.org/training-partnership-recognized-white-house-expansion-apprenticeship-program (accessed December 5, 2014).

being developed, primarily under the ACA, will not happen without investment in this key workforce, Stone said.

CARE COORDINATION AND THE CONSUMER VOICE

Henry Claypool
American Association of People with Disabilities

The agencies that provide personal care services in the Medicaid environment operate on thin margins, and managed care organizations are
expanding in this area, increasingly affecting how states deploy their home-
and community-based service systems. Claypool sees an opportunity to help
these organizations understand the importance of the direct care workforce.
It would be a fundamental error for them to adopt a "rigid clinical frame"
and deploy resources solely on the basis of a medical model, he said. If
they did, the provision of any service outside medical care—that is, all the
social services needed by patients with chronic medical conditions and their
families—would be deemed a service that increases costs.

Among the many changes in the health care environment in recent years
are the consumer-directed workforce and the independent living movement,
both of which involve the provision of care in the home. According to
Claypool, research shows that a majority of older adults want more control
over the workers who come into their home, including when they come
and what they do. Programs that offer this greater control are consumer
directed. The independent living philosophy can help guide the thinking
about how this workforce is deployed and how people with clinical training can guide that process. Independent living services provide services
related to ADLs. They are important functional tasks and, in the Medicaid
world, are distinct from clinical tasks. "We have to think about this as not
skilled versus unskilled, which is a framing that I think is harmful to the
workforce," he said.

The idea of career ladders is grounded in the skilled care frame and
considers home care workers to be the bottom rung. However, Claypool
said, "we should value that role and invest in it appropriately. We are
actually adding value by helping people remain direct care workers." The
promotora[6] model, he believes, can be adapted to enable direct care work-

---

[6] A *promotora* is a community health worker used in Hispanic communities. "As trusted
members of their community, *promotoras* provide culturally appropriate services and serve
as a patient advocate, educator, mentor, outreach worker, and translator. They are often the
bridge between the diverse populations they serve and the health care system" (Rural Assistance Center, 2015).

ers to take on as much responsibility as they possibly can to assist people with chronic conditions and difficulties with ADLs.

Encouraging direct care workers to expand in these areas can be done in ways that complement nurses' roles, freeing registered nurses to practice at the top of their training and scope of practice, he said. The *promotora* model also embodies the idea of health promotion, reinforcing the "independent living philosophy and values that come with it, [which] are essential to allowing the workforce to really understand how they can work with individuals."

In addition, he suggested that attention be given to health-promoting activities related to diet and exercise. Direct care workers from the same socioeconomic strata as their clients understand the challenges faced by people who live in food deserts, who are unaccustomed to balanced meals, or who have no good options for exercise. Even helping a person develop the strength to walk to the bus stop can be helpful. (Claypool noted that knowledge of how to navigate fixed-route public transportation systems encourages independence, because they are more reliable than paratransit systems.) Direct care workers can potentially serve as "force multipliers," he said.

QUESTIONS AND COMMENTS

An open discussion followed the panelists' presentations. Workshop participants were able to give comments and ask questions of the panelists. The following sections summarize the discussion session.

Education and Training

Margherita C. Labson, The Joint Commission, asked how prepared the professional staffs of home health agencies are to conduct the types of training suggested for direct care workers. Stone said that she does not believe that they are trained in this at all. Stone cited a 2008 Institute of Medicine (IOM) report that addressed a lack of training in geriatric competencies across the entire workforce (IOM, 2008). She said that a systemic lack of investment has produced a shortage in the number of faculty to be trained, with home care receiving the least investment of all. Claypool said that organized labor has stepped forward in a number of states, like Washington, to develop a training infrastructure.

Michael Johnson, BAYADA Home Health Care, said that a bit of an "educational arms race" is under way. He noted that all physical therapists, occupational therapists, and pharmacists are now (or will be) trained at the doctoral level. He asked if health care professionals are becoming overeducated to do some of the things that they used to do. Is there someone who can do the work just as well for less? Johnson answered his own question, saying that direct care workers can perform many tasks.

Engaging Individuals and Their Families

Johnson also raised concerns about engaging the family in care. If the family's perception is that the only person who can do the job is a clinician with a doctoral-level education, he said, problems arise. Family caregivers are disempowered; they do not believe that they can do the tasks required of them. Another consequence of this trend, Claypool said, is that it may be more difficult to integrate teams in which some members have obtained their advanced degrees and others have little formal training. Members of the team with little formal training may have additional and long-standing socioeconomic disadvantages and cultural differences with other team members, as well, yet their perspectives can be of great value because their backgrounds reflect the backgrounds of patients and families. "When we wake up to this one day, I hope we have not disempowered them to such an extent that they no longer share their wisdom," Claypool said.

George Taler, Washington Hospital Center, asked if, when the VA enrolls someone in the home-based primary care program, a mechanism is in place for assessing the ability and willingness of caregivers in the home to provide care, the caregivers' integration with the service community, and the household's financial resources that can be directed to care. According to Edes, the VA's home-based primary care program does not require that veterans have a caregiver in the home. Any assessment of questions of this type would be made by the social worker or nurse. The VA also has a good track record with finding people in the community who want to be caregivers under the medical foster home model. Gail Hunt said that a number of assessment tools have been developed to determine the ability and willingness of family caregivers to perform needed tasks. The basic criteria have been identified, but no universal tool exists, and it is not clear how widely these basic criteria are used. Part of "ability," she indicated, depends on what the tasks are and the physical or time limitations of the caregiver. In addition, Claypool said, at some point it may be useful to assess the willingness and ability of patients to adopt the use of technology, as home-based diagnostic and treatment options are rapidly expanding, but many older adults believe that technology is difficult to use, he said.

Teams of Care

Johnson further asked about what has been done to help teams be successful, so that the people who are accustomed to being the leaders and somewhat expected to take that role—primarily physicians—have the competency to know when to lead and when to follow. Do direct care workers, who also should be part of the team, feel competent enough to lead, or do they always follow? Edes said that to address some of the dynamics that arise in interdisciplinary teams, the VA conducts interdisciplinary team training. In addition, every team member takes a leadership role on a rotating basis. The home-based primary care providers are the VA staff, and they rely on community providers for home health aide and hospice services. It can be harder to embrace these non-VA staff as team members. At the same time, Edes believes that involving family caregivers in the development of care plans has helped them integrate with the care teams. In a home care housing program under way in Camden, New Jersey, Stone said, a *promotora*/community health worker model is being used. In that model, the *promotora* is doing most of the frontline work, including medication management and involving patients in chronic disease self-management. These staff are working effectively with the rest of the team. "They are communicating with each other all the time," and it is not high-tech.

Technology and Services

Kathryn H. Bowles, Visiting Nurse Service of New York Research Center and the University of Pennsylvania School of Nursing, asked about the key features that make the VA telehealth program work while others across the nation struggle with making it cost- and clinically effective. Edes said that although he is not responsible for the VA telehealth programs, his department does integrate with those efforts, which serve about 15 percent of veterans receiving home-based primary care. Telehealth appears to work well, he said, when the home care team and telehealth team meet regularly and solve problems together. This kind of effective integration boils down to good communication. Bowles asked if having one electronic health record across the entire VA system helps. Edes responded that in any kind of emergency situation, like Hurricane Katrina or even when veterans travel from one part of a state to another, it is tremendously valuable.

Judith Stein, Center for Medicare Advocacy, asked what can be done to close the divide between the people who need home care services and the people who provide them. Claypool believes that the home care worker minimum wage and overtime protection rules recently put on hold by the U.S. Department of Labor will "live to see another day," in part out of growing recognition of how much home-based LTSS depends on these workers. Finally, Stein noted that many of the services that have been discussed at the workshop are vitally important but are being inappropriately denied coverage under Medicare.

6

Models of Care and
Approaches to Payment

No single model of care will be able to meet the needs of all individuals who receive (or want to receive) home health care. As a variety of approaches are needed to deliver a range of services in the home, different approaches to payment also need to be considered. At the workshop, an overview of the current range of models and approaches to payment was provided, and then six speakers described their individual experiences (including both successes and challenges) in trying new models of care and using new approaches to payment. Together, these presentations consider how to facilitate the development of the models and payment approaches that will be needed to achieve a vision for the future role of home health care.

OVERVIEW OF THE RANGE OF MODELS
AND APPROACHES TO PAYMENT

Peter Boling
Virginia Commonwealth University

Boling began his presentation by describing the scenes that he encounters when he takes his medical students to his patients' homes, an aspect of clinical training that students rarely experience. Recent visits provided an opportunity for the students to see the deep connections that can develop between clinician and patient, he said. These stories, presented in Box 6-1, gave the students—and the workshop participants—a sense of the continuum of care and the diverse realities of patients' worlds.

BOX 6-1
Two Virginia Men

Boling took his medical students to the home of a Virginia man, age 53 years, who has lost the use of his limbs and torso. He has been Boling's patient for 20 years. He spends his days mostly in the prone position because that gives him the most maneuverability, given his limited use of his hands. As a result, he developed pressure ulcers on his elbows. He has had multiple hospitalizations because of urinary tract infections. On one occasion, he was placed in a nursing home, after which he said he is never going back. He is heavily dependent on medical technology, specifically, his bed and wheelchair.

This man runs a consumer-directed care model for himself. According to him, the three women assigned to comanage his care with him are not very competent, and he has had to teach them what to do. In fact, he has trained a number of different individuals to be his aides and how to properly care for a quadriplegic, "which is not easy," Boling said.

The second patient Boling described is a man who was accidentally shot in the neck at age 16 years while walking with his sisters on Coney Island. He completed his college education, obtained a master's degree, and became an effective teacher. One of his students is the sister of the woman who is now his personal care aide (again, a consumer-directed care arrangement), and she—along with her baby and husband—live in the front part of the house where he stays. She smokes a lot. Although it is not an ideal situation, he has been homeless in the past, so it is much better than what he has experienced at some other times in his life.

He has a laptop and is waiting for Internet service. Boling wants to help him reconnect with his teaching. In the past, this man also trained some of his aides, who at night worked in strip tease clubs. He says that was a very interesting period for him and that they actually did a pretty good job.

SOURCE: As presented by Peter Boling on September 30, 2014.

Measuring the Value of Home Health Care

The diversity of home health care experiences makes the components of care as well as their effects hard to measure in a reliable, consistent manner, "so that you can say structure, process, [and] outcome and be able to categorize them in a way relevant to federal health policy," Boling said. Nevertheless, it is necessary to define the population of care recipients and their needs in some manner. The really complicated patients—analogous to Thomas E. Edes's 5 percent—simply do not fit into the usual care systems. "We need to carve these patients out," Boling said, and provide them care by use of a different model in which care is paid for differently and outcomes are measured differently.

Boling said that a strong medical component is often left out of home health care and that it needs to be combined with social supports into a service that is truly patient-centered and affordable and that aligns funding with the care model. When quality is measured and value is estimated, it is important to adjust the cost estimates according to the risks for the population being served and to select quality measures specific to that population, as well as the care setting. These measures must be simultaneously accurate and not too burdensome to collect, he said.

Patient Needs

Home health care users fit into a variety of subtypes, Boling said (see Table 6-1). The most complicated, challenging, and expensive patients receiving home health care, Boling said, are those with a high comorbidity and illness burden who may need acute care at home, post-acute transitional care, or long-term health care. His estimates are that some 3 million to 4 million Americans are chronically limited to their homes and have three or more problems with activities of daily living (ADLs). Most but not all of them are elderly, he said, and although they may have a reduced life expectancy, they are not necessarily eligible for hospice. Some are dependent on medical technology, such as ventilators. A group of very ill patients—another 2 million to 3 million—also requires large amounts of medical care, but only for a relatively short time, because of an acute illness or injury or because of an advanced life-limiting condition.

TABLE 6-1 Home Health Care User Categories

Category	Description of Home Health Care User
A	The user has no illness (acute or chronic) and uses self-help sources
B	The user is ambulatory, independent, and not "sick"; some chronic health conditions exist
C	The user is younger, and functions (ADLs) are limited by one condition; the user is not "sick" often but needs continuous ADL support
D	The user is older with chronic cognitive or functional impairment; the user is infrequently acutely ill (low cost) and needs support with ADLs
E	The user requires post-acute care at the end of a discrete illness episode but has a rapid return to stable condition and home health care ends
F	The user has a high comorbidity and illness burden and is sick, and the cost of care is high

NOTE: ADLs = activities of daily living.
SOURCE: Reprinted with permission from Peter Boling, Virginia Commonwealth University.

Although the medical needs of these patients may be considerable, Boling said, they also need a matrix of social services, including, as other presenters have said, paid personal care, transportation, nutrition and home safety services, communication assistance, and legal and financial planning. The care system needs to make the services that cannot be provided by friends and family accessible, comprehensive, and coordinated and to make sure that these services are aligned with the patient's goals and needs, he said.

Medicaid recipients needing home health care encounter a program that, Boling said, offers discontinuous skilled care, a weak medical model, a slow response to urgent problems (resulting in unnecessary hospitalizations), and inconsistent attention to needs for help with ADLs and a system that is not aligned with other programs and payers, notably, Medicare.

Models of Home-Based Care

As evidence that substantial improvements are possible, even for acutely ill individuals, Boling pointed to a number of programs, in addition to the programs previously described by Edes sponsored by the U.S. Department of Veterans Affairs (VA) (see Chapter 5). Boling reviewed evaluations of three models of care that have proved successful according to patient outcomes and cost reductions but that have not been adequately replicated or scaled up:

- An evaluation of Outcome-Based Quality Improvement, a 1990s performance improvement methodology that reduced hospitalizations by about one-quarter (Shaughnessy et al., 2002);
- A randomized trial of Hospital at Home, which provided hospital-level care at home and that resulted in fewer medical complications and lower costs (Leff et al., 2005); and
- A randomized trial of the effects of assignment of an experienced nurse practitioner (NP) to at-risk older adults while they were still in the hospital; the NP followed up with these adults once they were home, managed their care, and ensured that the care plan was followed; this approach resulted in reduced hospital readmissions and a 50 percent cost savings (Naylor et al., 1999).

Concerns that have limited the spread of these highly targeted programs are that they are not considered scalable, which is not necessarily true, Boling said. A key question is who benefits from the savings from such programs? Although they are good for the Medicare program, participating hospitals experience reduced reimbursements. Boling tells his hospital and the subspecialists who practice there, "You will not miss these patients if we carve them out. You lose money on them. They clog up the works and slow down the clinics." Finally, not all patients in the NP-centered program described above could function without additional help after the NP visits end. "That's a limitation of this new silo—the transitional care silo—that we are starting to create," he said. Stimulated by this problem, a less expensive, less intensive intervention was tested on a slightly less sick group of patients and also proved effective, but it provided lower cost savings (Coleman et al., 2006). This model involved patient empowerment, improved communication and records transfer, and had "a lighter clinical touch," Boling said. Although it may be more easily scalable, the problem of who will pay for it remains.

Boling then reviewed a number of other innovative programs.

Community-Based Care Transitions Program

The Community-Based Care Transitions Program,[1] created under Section 3026 of the Patient Protection and Affordable Care Act of 2010 (ACA),[2] has devoted up to $500 million to tests of new transitional care models at more than 100 participating sites so far. Again, this program provides short-term assistance for patients, Boling said, but the program "starts to reorient people's thinking in the community and involves a lot more people in the process of improving health care."

Geriatric Resources for Assessment and Care of Elders

The Geriatric Resources for Assessment and Care of Elders (GRACE) model was tested in a randomized trial and showed considerable improvement in clinical care processes (Counsell et al., 2007). Selected patients were discharged home, where they received quarterly visits from an NP for 2 years. The NPs reported back to clinic-based geriatricians and made recommendations. Analysis showed an approximately 30 percent reduction in overall costs, attributable to fewer hospitalizations and emergency room visits in the highest-risk subgroup, Boling said.

---

[1] See http://innovation.cms.gov/initiatives/CCTP (accessed December 24, 2014).

[2] Patient Protection and Affordable Care Act of 2010, Public Law 111-148, 111th Cong., 2nd sess. (March 23, 2010).

Program of All-Inclusive Care for the Elderly

The Program of All-Inclusive Care for the Elderly (PACE)[3] is an established benefit for individuals dually eligible for Medicare and Medicaid
that has been used by only a small number of participants (Wieland et al.,
2010). It requires people to give up their traditional Medicare and Medicaid
and enter a structured, high-overhead, mostly center-based program providing comprehensive health and social services. Although the savings that
it achieves are modest, Boling said, the quality of services for those who
like the model is high, and it decreases the cost burden for government
programs by accepting the full risk for enrollees.

Home-Centered Primary Care

Boling noted a non-VA home-centered primary care program tested in
a case-control study that used an interdisciplinary team model to provide
medical care and hospice services in the home (De Jonge et al., 2014). This
model achieved better care and reduced costs 17 percent over 2 years and
reduced costs 31 percent for the most complex, sickest patients through
reductions in hospitalizations and nursing home use. It requires an experienced care team, and traditional fee-for-service payments do not cover its
costs.

Independence at Home

Independence at Home,[4] funded by Section 3024 of the ACA, is targeted to post-acute care patients with several serious chronic conditions and
disabilities. The participating sites, which are using various organizational
models, may be able to share in program savings. This is a key, Boling
said, to creating incentives for medical care providers to become involved
in longitudinal home-based care for a high-cost population and to fund
the program longer term. If the model works, legislation will be needed to
expand it.

Boling responded to a question from James Pyles of Powers Pyles Sutter
& Verville PC about how Independence at Home works for seriously chronically or terminally ill individuals who may need help on a 24-hour-per-day
basis. Realistically, Boling said, the only people in the home 24 hours per
day are patients and their family members. Then, depending on what they
can afford, an aide may be present for 8 hours or more. If someone truly

---

[3] See http://www.npaonline.org/website/article.asp?id=12&title=Who,_What_and_Where_
Is_PACE (accessed December 5, 2014).

[4] See http://innovation.cms.gov/initiatives/independence-at-home (accessed December 5,
2014).

needs care 24 hours per day, whether they are in hospice or getting to that point, the care process is often supported by a constellation of friends and family, neighbors, and paid aides under existing financial models, Boling said.

Further Considerations

Overall, Boling noted the following lessons from these models:

- Significant cost savings are achievable.
- Targeting of the highest-risk patients is the key to achieving savings.
- Transitional care models need to transition to longer-term care for many patients.
- To continue, successful models need stable sources of funding.

This litany of successful and promising programs also suggests the need to look at some models that have not worked. Lessons from these approaches, Boling said, include

- The coordination of care through a call center or the like does not work unless good integration with primary care is achieved.
- Patient-centered medical homes are not sufficiently patient centered for the sickest people who are homebound, although they may be effective for the majority of patients.
- Accountable care and managed care models need some kind of a carve out for the frailest population.

Standards of care that recognize that some of the treatments that make sense in younger, healthier populations may not be relevant to frail individuals who are in their 80s and 90s are needed, Boling said. In some cases, these treatments do not save lives or improve outcomes and instead create troubling side effects and increase risk. Low-value services are too expensive at almost any price point, he concluded.

Teresa L. Lee, Alliance for Home Health Quality and Innovation, asked how the system can navigate toward new delivery models that make more optimal use of comprehensive home health care without setting up more silos. Boling advocated for carving out this population from the hospitals and clinics and bringing in a well-trained home health care workforce to deliver team-based care using an integrated medical-social model.

EXPERIENCE OF SUTTER HEALTH

Jeffrey Burnich
Sutter Health

Sutter Health is a large, not-for-profit integrated delivery system in Northern California. Like other providers, Sutter faces the urgent need to transform its care delivery practices across the health care continuum to better serve very frail, very sick, very-high-cost patients, particularly in the last few months of life, Burnich said. Many, but not all, of these patients are Medicare beneficiaries. In doing so, one of Sutter's greatest challenges, Burnich said, has been system fragmentation.

In 2009, Sutter Health developed the Advanced Illness Management (AIM)[5] program by bringing together a cross-disciplinary group (including doctors, nurses, home health care and hospice professionals, and data analysts) to try to develop a new approach to integrating services for its home health care population. Burnich said that it built on Sutter's managed care experience and a strengthened telesupport system. The result was the creation of transition teams in the home-based care program and the capacity to respond to emergencies, such as acute exacerbations of illness, pain crises, and family anxiety for patients receiving either end-of-life care or other services. The integrated care system is organized around patients' goals and is targeted to people who are both frail and the sickest. Referrals can come from a hospital, a doctor's office, or a skilled nursing facility. Burnich noted that about 40 percent of the referrals come directly from physician practices, and "without the doctors' support, this program wouldn't be where it is today." The combination of AIM and integrated care management expertise in the home is yielding person-centered, evidence-based, coordinated care, he said.

The Sutter system uses a single electronic health record to record most of the services that it provides, although the home health care nurses use a separate database. The record system that Sutter uses also does not have a hospice platform, but Burnich believes that it will be adopted when it is developed.

About 2,100 patients are in this system at present, with the number increasing by about 5 percent per month, but the number of patients included is limited by the need to find trained home health care providers. The program leaders attribute this growth to the strong demand from physicians: "We can't keep up," Burnich said. Program staff make sure that they

---

[5] See http://www.sutterhealth.org/quality/focus/advanced-illness-management.html (accessed December 5, 2014).

communicate with referring physicians to assure them that their patients are receiving good care but do not inundate them with data.

According to Burnich, the following are essential parts of the program for each patient:

- An advance care plan,
- A self-management plan for patients of symptoms that raise a red flag,
- Medication management,
- Ongoing follow-up visits, and
- Engagement and self-management support.

All of this, he said, rests on a curative plus palliative care foundation.

The Sutter project received a health care innovation grant from the Centers for Medicare & Medicaid Services (CMS), and at the time of the workshop, Burnich was preparing to present its preliminary results to that agency. These include a 59 percent reduction in hospitalizations for patients enrolled in the AIM program for 90 days, a 19 percent reduction in emergency department use, and a 67 percent reduction in high-cost days in intensive care units. Significant cost savings attach to each of these reductions.

Initially, Burnich said, hospital administrators thought that they did not want to lose these patients because they contribute to the hospital's fixed costs ("contribution margin"), but in fact, after day 9 or 10, they cost the hospital more than the reimbursement covers, creating negative income. By keeping these high-cost patients at home, hospitals actually make more money by losing less. When the staff in the finance department understand that, they are more comfortable with a program that does not fill beds, Burnich said.

Sutter has analyzed the profit and loss implications of the program for hospitals, for doctors' practices (because they might lose revenue), and for home hospice, Burnich said. The doctors actually benefit financially from it, because there is no other way to cover the high cost of caring for these patients and providing the lengthy consultations that they need. The savings amount to $11,000 per beneficiary per year, and over the 3 years of the CMS grant, Burnich said, Sutter plans to serve 10,800 patients. It committed to save $29 million on these patients but is on track to actually save $118 million. The impetus for pursuing a program of this type arises because of the extent of capitation within Sutter, which means "we are on the hook for managing these patients," Burnich said.

EXPERIENCE OF ATRIUS HEALTH

Richard Lopez
Atrius Health

Atrius Health is a nonprofit alliance of six leading independent medical groups in eastern Massachusetts that has created an integrated delivery system that includes both home health care agency and hospice services. Atrius Health provides care for 1 million adult and pediatric patients. The Visiting Nurse Association Care Network and Hospice (VNACNH), which has been part of the system for the past few years, is a wholly owned subsidiary, and Lopez said that its integration with the rest of Atrius's providers is an ongoing process. This acquisition was deemed necessary to take care of the alliance's capitated patients through Medicare Advantage, its accountable care organization (ACO) patients through the CMS Pioneer program, and, ultimately, Lopez said, its commercially insured patients. About 35,000 Atrius patients are involved with its Pioneer ACO, and some 25,000 are enrolled in Medicare Advantage. Together, they account for a half billion dollars in risk. The demographic trends and illness projections mentioned by previous workshop speakers are very relevant to Atrius's strategic planning, Lopez said.

One strong point in acquiring VNACNH, Lopez said, was that its geographical coverage area was relatively congruent with that of Atrius. The availability of both physician services and services from VNACNH allowed Atrius managers to plan effectively and be financially aligned to serve a large, high-risk population. To do that, Lopez said, Atrius has created interfaces that

- Improve communication between home health care providers and physician offices;
- Foster teamwork across providers and disciplines;
- Facilitate the development of a collaborative program designed to meet patient-centered care goals, regardless of payment source; and
- Provide metrics for accountability.

Communication and Teamwork

Although the visiting nurses complete the usual lengthy intake forms that assess patients for everything from the risk of falls to the medications that they take and the presence of depression, these records are often not well incorporated into the patients' records, Lopez said. Atrius's electronic health records system ensures that current assessments appear where they are convenient for physicians to access. Practice care managers receive a weekly email report on clinical data for active patients. The report includes progress toward goals, response to teaching, discharge planning, and any hospice team meeting notes. The report is then distributed to physicians. (Lopez noted that the Atrius system uses encrypted email for communication among providers.)

Atrius has instituted an automated referral system through the electronic health records, so that when a referral is made it goes to VNACNH intake staff, who can then access the patient's record to set up the case for VNACNH. At present, VNACNH uses an end-of-life information system, and Lopez said that Atrius is considering adopting a home health care module in the next year or two to make records more fully integrated.

A steering committee comprising senior staff oversees the development of the Atrius-VNACNH relationship and clarifies policies and procedures to ensure care coordination and collaboration, Lopez said. In addition, many specific activities have been undertaken to transform VNACNH's relationship with Atrius Health from one in which VNACNH is a vendor to one in which VNACNH and Atrius have a true partnership.

In primary care practices, Lopez noted that an effort has been made to integrate members of the patient-centered team with VNACNH staff in relevant places along the continuum of care. In particular, work has concentrated on educating practice staff about palliative care and end-of-life challenges, he said. Another specific team-building strategy is "geriatric roster reviews," which are regular team meetings in the doctor's office in which case reviews are done for patients identified to be at high risk.

Program Design and Metrics

VNACNH has developed a palliative care consult team that works with the primary care practice and the home health care staff to better manage patients near the end of life, and it also has a robust advance care planning program. According to Lopez, one goal of the end-of-life efforts is to encourage earlier hospice enrollment, contrary to current practice patterns in Massachusetts, which overall has one of the nation's shortest hospice lengths of stay. "A lot of low-hanging fruit is there," Lopez said, as Atrius attempts to improve quality and reduce costs of care.

The system has developed a one-time-visit home assessment system paid for not through Medicare but by the physician groups. They assess patients' homes for safety and adequacy as a care environment. Atrius's total joint program, also paid for by the physician groups, enables patients to undergo rehabilitation at home rather than in a skilled nursing facility or inpatient rehabilitation facility. Those who can go home with help after knee or hip replacement incur about $3,500 less in care costs and have the same or better outcomes, Lopez said.

Lopez also noted that by using the programmatic flexibility allowed under the Pioneer ACO program, Atrius's VNACNH staff help patients who end up in the emergency department go home with support rather than experience an unnecessary hospital admission or referral to a skilled nursing facility.

According to Lopez, other program initiatives in some stage of planning or initial implementation include the following:

- Expansion of telehealth care for congestive heart failure patients beyond the Medicare episode;
- Implementation of physician/VNACNH visits by video and through the use of remote diagnostic technology; and
- Expansion of home-based primary care, which entails streamlined communication and scheduling as a team.

The philosophy underlying all these programs is one of care management and not medical management, Lopez said, and home visits are based on need, not insurance coverage.

The results of this integration of home health care and Atrius Health's physician practices are being assessed monthly through the use of measures examining cost and utilization, quality, and the patient experience. Lopez said that the data collected for the Pioneer ACO and Medicare Advantage patients receiving VNACNH home health care services indicate that in comparison with the outcomes in previous years,

- Hospital readmission rates are down;
- VNACNH is providing an increasing proportion of home health care;
- Eighty-five percent of patients admitted to VNACNH are screened for the risk of falls and for depression (with the outcome of the screening being documented in the electronic record); and
- Ninety percent of patients have had a discussion about medicines, pain management, and home safety.

According to Lopez, work still needs to be done to increase the proportion of patients with advance care planning discussions and documentation and to improve patient satisfaction (84 percent of patients give the VNACNH a rating of 9 or 10).

In the future, Atrius Health is considering developing an internal bundled payment system, providing clinical pharmacy management in the home, and more fully integrating home health care and hospice services with the system's existing medical record system. The system will continue to work on its major challenge, Lopez said, of "bridging that communication gap between the doctor's office and the home."

EXPERIENCE OF THE VISITING NURSE SERVICE OF NEW YORK

Rose Madden-Baer
Visiting Nurse Service of New York

The Visiting Nurse Service of New York (VNSNY) is the nation's largest not-for-profit home health care organization, Madden-Baer said. It offers home health, hospice, and palliative care; Medicare Advantage; a managed long-term care plan; paraprofessional and private duty nursing; and aide services. On any given day, she said, approximately 66,000 people are under the agency's direct or coordinated care, and in 2013, its staff made some 2.3 million clinical visits for patients of all ages.

VNSNY is involved in a number of acute, post-acute, and community-based care models for population health, and according to Madden-Baer, the agency has a dual imperative to transform itself from not only providing excellent home health services to also using its expertise to develop centers of excellence around care coordination and to provide new models of care as alternative payment structures develop. "We use our care coordination expertise as a laboratory for development and testing of new community-based health care models," Madden-Baer said. The vision is to be the region's best-in-class not-for-profit community-based integrated delivery system so that it may play a role well beyond that of a traditional home health care agency.

VNSNY Platform

The platform that VNSNY has developed is used for the coordination of population care, management of delegated care, and population health, depending on the needs of particular programs or clients. The platform covers the following:

- Evidence-based tools;
- Person-centered goals and care plans;
- Nurse-conducted assessment and care coordination;
- Health coaching and support;
- Collaboration with primary care and other providers;
- Financial and clinical outcomes measurement and reporting; and
- Predictive analytics and risk stratification.

At the center of all these activities is the individual patient and his or her family, Madden-Baer said, whom VNSNY staff interact with in multiple ways: face-to-face, by telephone, and electronically. These interactions are based on a person-centered goal and care plan that includes opportunities, goals, and interventions.

A set of predictive analytics has been developed with the agency's research center. These tools allow the stratification of patients into low-risk, rising risk, and high-risk categories. The type of risk may vary, she said, from risk for hospitalization to risk for care management, for example. The agency uses a care management documentation system (not a home health care documentation system) that includes a comprehensive health risk assessment and also has the New York State–mandated uniform assessment tool embedded in the system. Data from the risk assessments contribute to the calculation of the risk score. Madden-Baer said that once a person is appropriately categorized, the agency uses a "dosed mix" of interventions and evidence-based tools to improve patient activation, depression symptoms (as applicable), and medication adherence.

Workforce

Madden-Baer noted that patient assessments are performed by registered nurses (RNs) who are trained in a 12-week intensive program at the Duke University School of Nursing to be population care coordinators. Their training modules cover topics such as care transitions, evidence-based practices, social determinants of health, health literacy, sociodemographics, and biopsychosocial issues. The RN population care coordinators lead teams that include NPs, psychiatric NPs, pharmacists, hospital-based RN liaisons (who, in some cases, serve as transitional care coordinators), social workers, and health coaches. In addition, they work with a wide range of other health care providers and organizations as needed.

The health coaches, who are trained in Eric Coleman's Care Transitions Model, not only provide health coaching and patient navigation but may also accompany high-risk patients to their first primary care appointment and ensure that patients understand the medical terminology and patient-provider discussion. The health coaches can help address health literacy barriers, Madden-Baer said, because they often come from the same community as the patient or speak the same foreign language.

New Projects

VNSNY is engaged in two CMS demonstration projects on bundled payments, Madden-Baer said, and is embarking on a hospital-at-home project with a large academic medical center. Some health plans have delegated their disease management services to VNSNY, for example, for diabetic and prediabetic enrollees. The agency is working with ACOs and health plans to provide posthospitalization transitional care. It has two projects under way to provide health and wellness services with behavioral health support for posttraumatic stress disorder and reconnections to primary care services for people affected by Hurricane Sandy. VNSNY also provides care coordination for the largest managed long-term care plan in the state.

New York State has sponsored a major initiative, the Delivery System Reform Incentive Payment Program, to encourage care coordination, attention to social determinants of health, behavioral health, and better management of services for Medicaid recipients and recipients dually eligible for Medicare and Medicaid. Madden-Baer said that at present VNSNY is partnering on at least 11 different projects, drawing on the agency's expertise in population health and the coordination of care.

Successes and Challenges

According to Madden-Baer, factors that have been important to the success of the agency are the use of evidence-based tools, commitment to staff training at all levels, a partnership with a leading academic institution to conduct training, the use of standardized approaches across service lines, and the use of interventions tailored to the specific needs of patients.

The agency's challenges, said Madden-Baer, are the current reimbursement model, the need to change the perception of VNSNY—internally and externally—to recognize that it is more than a home health care agency, and the need to capture data for program monitoring and evaluation.

EXPERIENCE OF HUMANA AT HOME

Eric C. Rackow
Humana At Home

According to Rackow, Humana is pivoting from a health plan to a health care company, creating an integrated care model to support its members. Humana At Home manages a suite of programs intended to provide care for older adults with multiple chronic conditions and functional, behavioral, or cognitive limitations. It has 60 home health care clinical offices in 13 states and almost 15,000 employed and contracted field care managers in its nationwide network. It has developed a national database that care managers can use to link members to local organizations that provide a range of supports, from Meals on Wheels to audio books for the blind and an online portal to support family caregivers. Rackow said that the program currently manages 600,000 Humana members who are in Medicare Advantage programs, Medicare Advantage special needs programs, or Medicare Advantage programs for individuals who are dually eligible for Medicare and Medicaid.

Pyramid of Services

The organization provides programs for managing individuals with an escalating intensity, depending on their functional and activity limitations as well as the number and severity of their illnesses (see Figure 6-1). Patient management starts with a telephonic program that offers in-home support when needed. About 25 percent of the population served by the telephonic program has an in-home visit to assess the home and the patient's circumstances, and about 10 percent has ongoing, in-home care management.

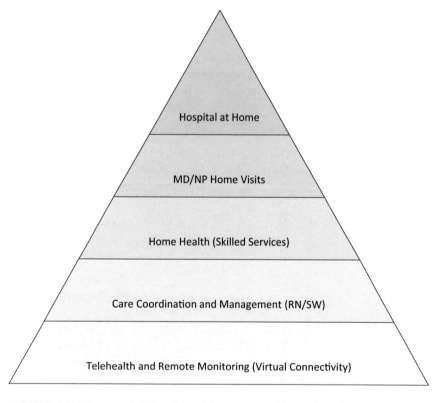

FIGURE 6-1 Humana At Home's goal for a range of home-based services.
NOTE: MD = medical doctor; NP = nurse practitioner; RN = registered nurse; SW = social worker.
SOURCE: Reprinted with permission from Eric Rackow, Humana At Home.

As other workshop presenters have emphasized, Rackow said that Humana At Home focuses its services on care coordination and management for the sickest 25 percent of members who drive almost 80 percent of the program's costs. "We are not going to solve this in the hospital," Rackow said. They target this population through the Humana At Home Chronic Care Program, which is an ongoing care management program for this population with critical needs, complex illnesses, and multiple chronic conditions. To identify the members most at risk for future severe illness, Rackow said, the organization looks at both the presence of chronic illnesses and functional limitations affecting ADLs. In Humana's experience, impairment of functionality "drives health care utilization and cost in the chronically ill, especially in seniors," Rackow said.

Humana's home health care pyramid begins on a base of telephone counseling, Rackow said, and then the middle levels of care use licensed home health aides to provide personal health care support. Furthermore, Humana is developing a program that provides skilled services that will be certified by Medicare. Care managers and members involved in the in-home personal and skilled care program have the additional support of community health educators, social service providers, behavioral management professionals, and an interdisciplinary care team of consultant nutritionists, pharmacists, and physicians.

At present, the top of the pyramid is the home delivery of physician services. This represents a distinct evolution from care coordination to direct clinical care. Ultimately, the organization sees developing these increasingly intense services all the way up to a hospital-at-home model. Humana At Home also offers a 30-day transitions program with three visits—one in the hospital before discharge, one within 48 hours of arriving home and before the primary care appointment, and a follow-up visit after that appointment. According to Rackow, at the time of his presentation at the workshop, some 30,000 Humana members had been served by that program.

Results

According to Rackow, 2013 data for the 116,000 members newly involved in care management showed a 42 percent decrease in hospital admissions, and the data for 2014 available to the time of his presentation showed a similar reduction. Among the 16,000 members participating in the posthospitalization transition program, 2013 data showed a 39 percent reduction in hospital readmissions, a decline that, again, was replicated in 2014, he said.

"But is keeping people out of the hospital the right thing to do?" Rackow asked. Humana data show that management at home not only is decreasing hospitalizations and readmissions but also is having a beneficial effect on patient mortality. Compared with the survival of matched control patients, those members involved in the chronic care program had a 2.8 percent absolute improvement in survival.

The country is in the middle of a paradigm shift, Rackow concluded, from a situation in which care is provided for acute conditions to one in which care is provided on a chronic basis, from a situation in which medical events trigger care to one in which medical events trigger holistic support, from a mind set in which health care is oriented toward a cure to one in which it is provided to enhance the patient's function, from fragmented care to integrated care, from a situation in which payment is provided per care episode to one in which payment is provided for a continuum of care, and from a situation in which care is provided in person to one in which it is provided virtually. A key element in this shift, he said, is the movement of the site of care from a hospital to the home.

EXPERIENCE OF OPTUM COMPLEX POPULATION MANAGEMENT

Ronald J. Shumacher
Optum Complex Population Management

Optum Complex Population Management is part of the UnitedHealth Group family of companies and a direct care delivery and care management business. (Other lines of business of Optum include data analytics, pharmacy benefits management, health care financial services, and consulting.) Like the other organizations that were described at the workshop, Shumacher said that Optum also serves a high-risk, vulnerable population that has high health care costs because of its utilization of hospital and emergency care. This population is poorly served by fragmented care and the lack of coordination of care for multiple chronic conditions and receives inadequate care at the end of life, he said. Typical Optum clients are managed care plans and, increasingly, programs for dually eligible individuals that delegate the delivery of services for their high-risk populations to Optum.

Although Optum has a range of programs for people who are in transition, have long-term service and support needs, or need palliative or end-of-life care, Shumacher focused his comments on Optum's Care Plus community program, a longitudinal home health care delivery model provided largely by NPs but with some services provided by physicians. Like the other programs described at the workshop, Optum uses data analytics to stratify patients on the basis of the risk of future service utilization and costs. "Essentially," Shumacher said, "we are providing a house call program with home-visiting providers that is paired with a care management and technology company to serve high-risk individuals."

The traditional approach within managed care for members with medically complex, multiple chronic conditions, Shumacher said, "really underperforms in a lot of ways." It entails numerous providers, patients receive many different medications, care is disjointed and confusing, and sometimes, elements of care plans are contraindicated or conflicting. Usually, he said, in-office medical care is insufficient both in time and in quality for these patients. Doctors do not receive the right insights, and patients do not develop the relationships with their clinicians required for the care of medically complex conditions.

In contrast, Shumacher said, Care Plus is a system that delivers clinical care and that is adaptable to all types of payers. It provides proactive, preventive maintenance and disease education services to teach people how to manage their care better. It uses care providers—NPs who work with the patients' primary care physicians—who can manage care in the home and write orders for laboratory tests and medications. They engage in advanced discussions with the patient about the patient's illness and explain different care options. A centralized care management team provides back office support.

The NPs specialize in having patients avoid unnecessary hospitalizations and emergency department visits. Similar to other models in various markets, Shumacher said, the baseline hospitalization rates for its population of patients are high but the use of in-home care services has helped achieve a reduction in hospital admissions of more than 60 percent. Furthermore, Care Plus can reduce overall health care costs for members with medically complex conditions by 42 to 52 percent compared with the costs for members whose care is not managed. In addition, as these extremely ill individuals approach the end of life, their rates of health care service utilization and costs are much lower than those for all Medicare patients, especially high-risk Medicare patients. In the last 6 months of life, Shumacher said, Care Plus can reduce costs by 61 percent. In addition, when they are asked to rate their satisfaction with the services of Care Plus, patients and families give Care Plus high scores.

In the future, in addition to working with managed care organizations, Care Plus could work with delegated provider groups, ACOs, and state and federal government programs, instead of only through health plans, Shumacher said. Care Plus is typically paid on a case rate per engaged member per month. However, it can be paid on a capitated basis, through a gain-sharing program with quality goals, and through a system in which some customers assume the full risk and take a percentage of the premium.

EXPERIENCE OF THE CAPABLE MODEL

Sarah L. Szanton
Johns Hopkins University School of Nursing

Szanton discussed the challenges faced by people with functional limitations that affect ADLs and how a project at the Johns Hopkins University School of Nursing works to improve function for many clients. (See Box 6-2 for a story related by Szanton.)

Szanton said that the Community Aging in Place—Advancing Better Living for Elders (CAPABLE) model[6] was developed with foundation and federal support and is now being tested under a Center for Medicare & Medicaid Innovation (CMMI) grant and through a randomized controlled trial funded by the National Institutes of Health. If these tests are successful, she said, the program may be implemented nationwide. "CAPABLE focuses directly on people's own functional goals, with the idea that if we address those, then they can take care of their medical issues," she said. It is client directed and not just client centered, and the clients' goals are exemplified by the following: "I want to be able to get up my stairs, so I can sleep in my bed instead of on my couch." Or, "I want to be able to stand long enough to be able to eat some foods, so I don't have to go back to the hospital."

Program Approach

By and large, program participants are low-income, dually eligible individuals recruited from community centers and mailings, but they are at high risk for functional limitations. CAPABLE provides clients with a team member who can make household repairs, a nurse, and an occupational therapist over 4 months. The initial visit is with the occupational therapist. In traditional home health care, occupational therapists cannot start a case, but in this model, function is the driver, and that is what occupational therapists address best, she said. They assess client needs for every ADL and instrumental activity of daily living (IADL), and then the clients prioritize those needs that they want to be addressed.

On the second visit, the occupational therapist goes through the whole house, examining all the areas that the client uses and assessing the causes of the client's limitations. The assumption is that "a limitation is a combination of what a person's qualities are and what the environment throws at them," Szanton said. "If you can give them grab bars or if you can fill in

---

[6] See http://nursing.jhu.edu/faculty_research/research/projects/capable (accessed December 24, 2014).

BOX 6-2
Mrs. B's Story

Baltimore, Maryland, resident Mrs. B has hypertension, congestive heart failure, diabetes, and arthritis. She was recently hospitalized for an exacerbation of her heart failure and just finished an episode of post-acute care in a skilled nursing facility. Like a cascade of dominoes, the precipitating heart failure problem occurred partly because she cannot stand up long enough to cook and cannot get groceries in the house. Therefore, she often eats some kind of prepackaged food, which tends to be a high-salt food, that she can just grab.

She keeps her clothes in her dining room, because that is where she lives. She can no longer climb the stairs to her bedroom. She cannot even really get dressed, because this "closet" is a sweater bag that is held together with safety pins, and her arthritic hands cannot undo the pins, Szanton said.

When first contacted by the CAPABLE program, Mrs. B was spending most of the day, every day, sitting in a chair. Holes in her floor made it dangerous to walk on. The Astroturf covering of the steps from the sidewalk to her front porch was ripped and hazardous. "None of us should walk up those front stairs," Szanton said, and certainly not someone with a shuffle, gait problems, and bad balance. Older adults who have lived in the same place for a long time and who do not have money to fix problems often similarly have houses that are starting to fall apart.

Although the expense associated with functional limitations is well-known, the impact of the home environment on people's function and how environmental improvements can reduce limitations in activities of daily living receive less attention. Mrs. B—and people like her—want to be more functional and often can be. CAPABLE program case management considered questions like the following: can she get her foot over the side of the bathtub, can she stand long enough to cook, and can she get dressed? These are often the issues that older adults care about more than their diseases, and these needs are mostly unaddressed.

What Mrs. B most wanted was to be able to stand long enough to make her meals. The CAPABLE program team tackled the problem: the nurse worked on her arthritis pain and her leg strength; the occupational therapist worked with her on the use of different cooking tools and ways to conserve energy; and the team member who made household repairs lowered the kitchen shelves, put in a microwave, and gave her a crock pot. These are simple steps, and all were related to achieving her goals.

SOURCE: As presented by Sarah Szanton on September 30, 2014.

---

the holes in their chair seats, sometimes they no longer have limitations." Together, the therapist and client fill out a work order for the person who will make household repairs, who tackles jobs in the client's priority order within a budget of $1,300. (Installation of a second banister is one of the most common requests, Szanton noted.)

At the end of the first month, the nurse starts. The nurse does not do anything about medication adherence, diet, or exercise unless it is the client's goal. The visits—six in total for the occupational therapist and four in total for the nurse—continue, with the occupational therapist and nurse working on a different goal at each visit. If a client has fewer goals, the program stops.

Results

The program has been pilot tested and may be ready to be scaled up, Szanton said. According to Szanton, the pilot tests showed that the one-time cost of the 10 professional visits averages $3,300 per enrollee, including travel, clinical care coordination, and home repair and modification. In contrast, nursing home care costs about $75,000 per year. If CAPABLE prevents even 3 weeks of nursing home care, she said, it has saved money; if it can avert hospitalization for one client in every five, it has saved money.

"As you can imagine," Szanton said, "the clients love it." One of the best program outcomes is decreased depression. Depression lifts because people can do what they want to be able to do, she said. For example, they can bathe themselves, they are cooking, and they are getting out of the house to go to church. "It's depressing to sit in a chair all day long." For most participants, the level of depression decreased or at least did not increase.

Rates of occurrence of functional limitations also followed a downward trend, Szanton said, with the number of functional limitations decreasing from an average of about four to about two, with almost 80 percent of clients seeing improvements in functional limitations and only 7 percent seeing declines. Szanton expects that stronger results would emerge with a post-acute care population.

In closing, Szanton described the following example. One client was taking 26 medications when she started the program. On the occupational therapist's first visit, it took 30 minutes for the client to walk the short distance from the bathroom to her bedroom, yet her goal was to go downstairs and wash her hair in the kitchen sink. "This shows the power of asking people what they want to be able to do," Szanton said.

QUESTIONS AND COMMENTS

An open discussion followed the panelists' presentations. Workshop participants were able to give comments and ask questions of the panelists. The following sections summarize the discussion session.

Policy and Payment

Lee asked the panelists what kinds of health policy changes are needed, particularly in Medicare, to facilitate the more appropriate use of home health care. For example, she asked, for those who received CMMI grants, were any Medicare rules waived? Rackow said that CMS needs to recognize functionality as an important component of keeping people healthy. At present, he said, Medicare does not reimburse for home health aide services that support beneficiaries' functional needs; it reimburses only for medical care, yet much health care utilization and cost are driven by those problems with function. Madden-Baer noted that for a congestive heart failure project that VNSNY is running with 50 hospitals, beneficiaries are not required to be homebound after the initial episode of care from a certified home health agency, as is usually required for subsequent care under the 90-day bundled payment. Also, the home health agency has the flexibility to engage a pharmacist consultant to simplify dosing schedules and to deploy NPs to the home when an appointment with a primary care physician is unavailable.

Boling suggested that the framework that focuses on chronic conditions be abandoned, because almost all elderly people have at least two chronic conditions. Instead, he said, the focus should be on function-limiting chronic conditions. He also advised that the expansion of the scope of various projects be managed, because if it is not, a project soon becomes unaffordable. The monitoring present under the CMMI grant helped Burnich's project avoid this tendency to expand. He said further that projects should not expand faster than the speed with which they can hire staff with the competence and skills to produce high-quality, reliable services. Rackow said that Humana has best practices and protocols that precisely define the amount of services, the time to be spent on those services, and the costs that the health plan pay per member per month, which, again, establishes boundaries.

Lee further asked what approaches to payment might be critical for future reforms. Capitated payments allow organizations to make the best decisions to support the health of their members, Rackow said. At present, access to a program like Humana's is limited to people enrolled in particular health plans and using particular provider groups. Shumacher said that programs that have strong results could be made more available to broader groups of people under a payment-for-value rubric.

Medicare Advantage is growing rapidly but under the ACA has built in some payment cuts that will discourage plans and providers from participating, Burnich said. Despite the advantages of capitation, not every senior will join Medicare Advantage, he said, and his organization is experimenting with other types of chronic care management programs.

Consolidation and Integration

A workshop participant asked if additional consolidation and integration of home, community, and post-acute care services will drive value. The participant further asked about the importance of integration in and of itself.

The company acquired by Humana that is now Humana At Home would never have been able to scale up its home health care program without being under the Humana umbrella, Rackow said, according to either its national coverage or the number of clients. Because of Humana's support, the Humana At Home program has expanded its horizons, seeing home health care as "the glue in the system" for keeping people as healthy as possible.

Lopez said that integration has been important to Atrius Health on multiple levels: alignment of mission and care delivery goals, provision of a financial bottom line, communication, and medical information sharing. Although Atrius could have worked with several visiting nurse associations in eastern and central Massachusetts instead of just one, he said, the alignment, goals, and financial and communications issues would have to have been worked out with each one of the associations and would have been burdensome.

The blurring of distinctions between providers and health plans, Burnich said, creates some risks. In the 1990s, plans that began serving as providers failed. The renewed trend "could be good," he said, "but we will have to see."

UnitedHealth Group's acquisition of INSPIRIS gave Optum increased ability to implement a successful delivery model that could reach many more payers and their members, Shumacher said. The bringing together of disparate businesses and the creation of a common platform take time, so it may be a while before the full value of integration can be realized, he said.

Madden-Baer said that VNSNY, being both a provider and a health plan, is learning to be "a lot less transactional and more care management focused" over the longer term. An example is the shift in the call center's approach: it supports the management of care when a patient calls, instead of instinctively advising patients to call 911 after hours.

Operating at a Smaller Scale

Terrence O'Malley, Massachusetts General Hospital, asked the panelists what lessons from their organizations can be applied to organizations that operate on a much smaller scale.

Telephone and telehealth care coordination, supported in various ways, can be scaled down, said Rackow. Humana is testing interactive voice response systems with patients with congestive heart failure.

Madden-Baer said that VNSNY's home health care program started small and thought of itself as a laboratory for testing models of care, which have been added over time and which have allowed the evolution of VNSNY into a much larger organization.

Technology is not the be-all and end-all, because "the warm touch is still a critical component," said Burnich, but there are ways to scale down through the use of technology, including through the use of sensory devices and video visits, for example.

A good first step for smaller agencies is to start tracking their data, Shumacher said. If they can show that they are providing better care, that quality is improving, and that costs are going down, they can grow from there. "A lot of what I talked about," Szanton said, "you can do for free." Just rephrasing the questions about function and asking the person about his or her goals are free. Home repair is going to provide such a strong return on investment that even with low levels of capitation, it can easily be provided. She suggested the mobilization of healthy older people who have skills, who have some time, and who may be eager to help fix up other people's homes.

7

Innovations in Technology

Technology is currently critical to home health care. Future advances in home health care technologies have the potential not only to facilitate the role of home health care within the overall health care system but also to help foster community-based independence for individuals. In one panel at the workshop, three speakers spoke about a wide range of technologies, including the existing base of evidence on the impact of technologies, the challenges facing the development and use of technologies for home health care, and how to facilitate the use of technology to achieve an ideal state of home health care in the future. Chapter 8 touches further on the role of information technology and the use of electronic health records.

EVIDENCE BASE FOR HOME HEALTH CARE TECHNOLOGIES

George Demiris
University of Washington

Computing is pervasive and ubiquitous, it is wearable, and it is used in every aspect of our lives, said Demiris. Advances in computing and information technology are also affecting home health care. Although information technology has been used in health care for a long time to bridge geographic distances and give people access to expert opinions without having to travel, ultimately, computing and information technology may actually be used to improve the quality of home health care services and enable their redesign, said Demiris. For example, Demiris noted that a MEDLINE search for papers on the use of technology in home health care published in 2003 found 556 papers; a decade later, the number was 1,390. Finally, not just the field of technology for home health care but also the evidence that goes with it have continued to grow, he said.

Active Versus Passive Technologies

One distinction that can be made among types of technologies is whether they are active or passive. Someone must operate an active technology, Demiris said, whether it is hardware or software. Active and passive technology can also be distinguished according to whether the user needs training. Passive technologies are, for example, cameras, sensors, or other devices embedded in the residential infrastructure that allow an individual to be monitored without requiring that individual or another person to operate them. As described in the literature, both types of technology have a variety of functions, Demiris noted, including monitoring and the provision of assistance in the various areas described in the following sections.

Physiological Monitoring

Active home telemonitoring devices can capture vital signs, weight, or symptoms and report them to a remote provider or a home health agency. Passive telemonitoring technologies include bed sensors that capture restlessness, sleep interruptions, or pulse and respiration during sleep.

Monitoring of Patient Function and Detection of Emergencies

Active technologies include devices that can detect falls and that people can wear. They also include personal emergency response systems that a person can also wear and that allow the person to press a button to summon help when he or she falls. Passive systems may be embedded in the carpet and can detect falls or near falls.

Safety

Alarm systems can actively detect fires or floods; passive systems can use motion and heat sensors, for example, to distinguish between heat that occurs during meal preparation and heat that builds up when a person turns on the stove and forgets about it.

Security

Camera systems allow the remote monitoring of residential spaces and visitors; passive systems use sensors to capture the level of activity and whether unusual patterns of activity are occurring.

Social Interactions

Social interactions can be made through the active use of social networks, and software can assess self-perceived social connectedness. Passive sensor-based systems track the number of visitors, the amount of time spent inside and outside the home, and sedentary behavior.

Cognitive and Sensory Activity

Active technologies can generate alerts and reminders, aid with the location of lost objects, or dispense medications. Passive automated features operate in the background and trigger warnings, alerts, and reminders or turn on lights.

The Evidence Base

Although both the amount and kind of evidence on home health care technologies are increasing—from evidence from pilot studies to evidence from some longitudinal research and randomized controlled trials—"it is still not really clear what seems to work and what doesn't work," Demiris said, especially because the findings are sometimes contradictory. The pace of technological advance is faster than traditional research grant cycles, so that by the time a study has been planned and funding has been acquired, the technology to be studied may be outdated. Furthermore, research projects rarely enable the tailoring of technologies on the basis of the situation in the home or the needs of the individual patient, because everyone in the study needs to receive the same intervention.

Technology interventions do not always have to be complex and sophisticated, Demiris said. Simple tools can sometimes be effective. For example, when the members of his group looked at ways to support informal hospice caregivers (e.g., family members, friends, neighbors), they used video conferencing technology to solve the caregivers' problems. This technology is being tested in a three-arm clinical trial with groups that receive (1) friendly visits and usual care (the controls), (2) standard care plus the problem-solving therapy in person, and (3) standard care plus the problem-solving therapy by video. If the results for Groups 2 and 3 are equivalent, the video intervention might be a cost-saving alternative. Although the cost results are not yet available, Demiris said that families are embracing the technology and "finding it [to be] a convenient and effective way to communicate" with the hospice teams.

Simple, low-cost technologies can allow health care workers to capture information more efficiently, and sometimes new technologies let them obtain new data, Demiris said. For example, traditional telehealth allows the capture of a person's blood pressure or weight, and some of the new technologies provide information about a person's lifestyle or behavior, eliminating the need to rely on self-reports.

One example of research on smart home technologies for people living in retirement communities involves the use of stove sensors, motion sensors, and sensors that detect water and electricity consumption, Demiris said. The last two are being used in an ongoing study to assess the overall mobility of people in their own homes. Now researchers also have data on sleep quality, restlessness, sedentary behavior, hygiene patterns, meal preparation, and so on. Again, these data should be much more accurate than those obtained from self-reports. Sophisticated algorithms may detect patterns of an individual's normal routine and deviations from those patterns, and clinicians can be presented with these summative data.

Usability and interface design are important considerations, especially for older adults, and technology designs need to be tested with these populations, Demiris said. For example, a multiuser kiosk used by people who wanted their vital signs assessed also asked them some questions, and researchers were challenged to create a system that could continuously tailor the interface to accommodate the functional, hearing, visual, or cognitive limitations of the users. Focus groups revealed that many older adults had visualization needs very different from those of their family members and clinicians, not only according to the type of information and level of detail desired but also according to the use of colors or features that one group found distracting and another group found helpful.

Studies that survey users about the acceptability of technologies may produce high levels of satisfaction, but Demiris believes that acceptance is more complex than that. For example, obtrusiveness is a broader concept than whether a system is active or passive. A technology may have undesirable features that are too psychologically or physically prominent. "Privacy is a huge issue, but it's not the only one," he said. The challenge of obtrusiveness is not only people's perceptions about what may happen to information about them but also the issue of function and how the equipment works, that is, whether it makes annoying noises or requires a lot of maintenance.

According to Demiris, other home technology issues need to be resolved, including

- Whether a technology will reduce the number of face-to-face visits;
- The technology's effects on the client's self-concept and the potential stigma of having it in the home ("turning the home into an ICU [intensive care unit]," one patient said);
- The technology's effects on people's daily routines;
- Whether any positive behavior changes are sustainable; and
- Affordability (in research studies, the technology is usually free).

In sum, although technology has a lot of potential and some evidence suggests that it can actually improve home health care services, "it's really about finding technology as a tool to meet clinical needs," Demiris said, rather than having it be "viewed as a solution to any of the problems we are facing."

ROLE OF TELEHEALTH

Raj Kaushal
Almost Family, Inc.

According to Kaushal, Almost Family, Inc., which was founded in 1976 and which operates in rural areas, is the fourth largest home health care provider in the United States, operating in 14 states and serving between 25,000 and 30,000 patients daily. Because of Almost Family's size, it can pilot test a variety of ways to improve care in its provider-based environment, and it works strategically with physicians, accountable care organizations, and hospitals.

A common denominator in the workshop so far, said Kaushal, is that in home health care technologies can be value-added services that aid with patient centeredness, sustainability, and reimbursement. Telehealth can have a wide range of complexity, from the simplicity of the telephone all the way to the extreme complexity of smart homes. Providers, however, do not know the best way to provide evidence-based telemedicine, he said. From the patient perspective, telehealth can range from being as simple as a telephone call, joining an online support group, or obtaining health information and self-management tools online to having email and online communication with health care providers. From the provider perspective, telehealth can range from the use of electronic health records and remote monitoring of vital signs and symptoms all the way to doing consultations and patient visits by video.

Technology can be helpful to teams of caregivers—physicians, nurses, therapists, social workers, and others, all of whom are delivering some aspect of care—by creating vital links that facilitate communication, coordination, and improved collaboration. Kaushal's organization tries to create those links within the company, as well as outside the company with the families, payers, external clinicians, and referral sources that it deals with every day.

Almost Family's goal, he said, is to keep patients independent in their homes, while reducing emergency care and hospitalizations and improving quality of life and perceived patient satisfaction, along with reducing the total cost of care. Almost Family does this not only by following an evidence-based medical care plan but also by paying attention to functional issues—ambulation, bathing, transfer, and so on—in what is a highly regulated industry.

Meanwhile, home health care takes care of people with complex and multiple chronic conditions (e.g., heart failure, chronic obstructive pulmonary disease, diabetes). Telehealth applications can enhance the management of this high-risk population, Kaushal said, by providing daily monitoring (between in-person visits), timely intervention as the patient's condition warrants, triage of clinical needs, and reinforcement of the treatment and discharge plan. The collaboration benefits include, for example, the ability to target visits and interventions to the patients and at times when they are the most needed and to tailor self-management training and health education for both patients and caregivers.

These patient management improvements assist physicians with both the coordination of care and the communication of health care problems and in the long run can save clinicians' time through improved coordination and collaboration, Kaushal said. For hospitals, they can reinforce the discharge plan, allow the hospital to recognize key indicators for readmission, contribute to the stabilization of patients after hospitalization, and generally support care transitions. The communication component encourages good communication and relationships with discharge planners.

For the system as a whole, telecommunications applications have the potential to gather and compile useful data so that health care systems can learn more about what home health care applications produce the most desired outcomes, Kaushal said. To test the impact of telehealth, his company worked with two of its partners, Medtronic and Cardiocom, on a 12-month study of some 566 patients with congestive heart failure. The intervention involved post-acute care and post-episode calls, used an interdisciplinary team approach, and created some champions in every study market. The study demonstrated the positive effects of telehealth on hospitalization rates and patient satisfaction and reduced 30-day hospital readmission rates to about half the national average (12.6 percent versus 24 percent nationally).

What Almost Family learned from this study, Kaushal said, was that it was not only technology or communication, coordination, and collaboration that made the difference but also the need to align staff, standardize care processes around clinical best practices, and then conduct focused training for clinicians around those processes. "Technology became a tool instead of a focus," he said. These best practices involved patient education as well.

According to Kaushal, positive outcomes like these can lead to organizational growth in several ways: by providing a competitive advantage, by enabling expansion of service coverage to other disease entities, and by creating opportunities for new business and new partnerships. Kaushal noted several lessons from the experience, including the following:

- Sites that had strong clinical care champions had the best outcomes.
- An integrated hospital–physician–home health care approach to the delivery of care produced the highest number of enrollees.
- Operational planning (program design; incorporation of new programs into ongoing operations; leadership support; broad stakeholder involvement; and definition of clear goals, timelines, and deliverables) is important.
- Vendor systems must be scalable.
- Monitoring of the communication between the members of the team and clinicians in the field directly improved patient care.
- A focus needs to be placed on communication that takes into account the situation, background, assessment, and recommendation (the SBAR approach).
- Success is different for different people, including different patients.

In the future, Kaushal believes that when standardization begins to occur and reimbursement is aligned with value, innovation will be accelerated if telehealth applications show that they can improve the quality of health care and not just save costs so that systems do not have to rely solely on local execution. "Because we live in the environment of reimbursement, if reimbursement is not there, sometimes good ideas fail," he said.

USE AND DEVELOPMENT OF ASSISTIVE TECHNOLOGY

Wendy J. Nilsen
National Institutes of Health

Nilsen reported on a workshop[1] held on September 9 and 10, 2014, at the National Institutes of Health (NIH) in collaboration with the Computer Community Consortium that explored technologies for aging in place and the gaps in products, policies, and research. The meeting was not about

---

[1] See http://www.cra.org/ccc/visioning/visioning-activities/aging-in-place/411-aging-in-place-workshop (accessed December 8, 2014).

"technology for technology's sake," Nilsen said; "technology is a reality." She pointed to Eric Dishman's visionary conception of health and the need to be thinking about the research that will point the way to that future. The workshop brought together health care researchers, technology researchers, industry, and government to discuss a series of questions around four topics:

1. How should technologies be designed for the aging population that wants to age at home? People who want to age in place are a diverse population, so should technologies be designed for the entire aging population or the 5 percent?
2. What kind of sensing innovations are needed? The design of sensors and the development of algorithms and precise timing to make them useful are tough, so what information should sensors be conveying?
3. How can people be helped to use technology to identify potential transition periods, and how can they be helped through health care transitions?
4. How can non–health care technologies be used to support health?

Nilsen noted that the workshop started from the assumption that technology could enhance health outside of hospitals and nursing homes by improving and sustaining health and increasing the quality of life; by allowing people to live at home longer; by reducing health care costs, especially the cost of unnecessary hospitalizations and rehospitalizations; and by reducing the strain on the health care workforce and on family caregivers. Further, the participants looked for ways to use technology's strengths to facilitate communication and data collection.

The workshop participants found that it was hard to talk to each other, Nilsen said. The people involved with technology wanted to see more investment in basic science, the people involved with health care wanted better technology now, and participants in general tended to focus on the technologies relevant to their own particular area of expertise. The technologists tend to think that all health care professionals are clinicians, she said, and the clinicians tend to think that all people involved with technology are programmers, but many partitions exist in both fields. "We really need to think about each other as complementary disciplines that work together for a common goal," she said.

Nilsen said that it will be necessary to transform thinking about home health care from an approach that it is "health care at home" to one in which it is "smart homes where people can be healthy." Technology in the home needs to be seen as an alternative form of care, she said, and not just an add-on to current systems. Such a rethinking implies a balance between personalization and universal design, as well as stronger human factors research to support that balance. She gave as an example the glucose monitor, saying that glucose monitors are often not designed for people who have diabetes because they have tiny buttons and even smaller type. "If you have problems with your vision from long-term diabetes, you can't see eight-point type," she said. The new technologies developed must be useful to the patient, the caregiver, and the care team by giving them actionable data useful to them, Nilsen said.

Other technologies that can serve everyone include, for example, tablet computers that have very simple operating systems for people who have never used computers. Furthermore, although users can take advantage of the health care applications that operate on tablet computers, they also can use the tablets for email and social networking. In other words, Nilsen said, the technology is designed so that people can use the technology in the way in which they intend to use it, with health care woven in. Ideally, integrated technologies free up time for conversation. For example, if home health aides did not have to take a blood pressure, she said, they might have time to find out what is going on in their patients' lives that may be having a greater impact on their health and well-being than their blood pressure.

For the long term, the health care system will need both more personalized technology and evidence-based, generalizable solutions that can be adapted to individual needs, Nilsen said. Other long-term considerations are the need to "future-proof" the technology—that is, the need to anticipate the rapid pace of technological change and not become stuck in what is possible today—and avoid the creation of new digital divides, in which only some people—for example, wealthier or better-educated individuals—can benefit, she said.

Another difficult question applies to monitoring technologies and, especially, cameras. Nilsen asked whether those technologies are there to keep an eye on the person so that the family knows what the individuals is doing and whether they are safe, or whether they are there to help the person be independent longer. This is one of the facets of obtrusiveness that George Demiris raised earlier.

Assessment of the usefulness of various technologies may require new research methods, such as "continuously evolving evaluations where technology can be evaluated on the fly," Nilsen said. Randomized clinical trials may still have a place for the evaluation of specific outcomes and the development of best practices. According to Nilsen, the following developments are needed to evaluate the evidence:

- New robust methods of analysis and sensor-driven decision analysis to create predictive, personalized models of health;

- Methods for rapidly generating evidence that will allow validation of the effectiveness and reliability of technologies, including addition of technology into existing trials or cohort studies;
- Test beds that will enable the efficient, economical, and systematic exploration of the use of technologies and that will involve the community in research;
- Development of a generalized matrix for cost analysis that uses, for example, the amount of the caregiver's time that is saved as one of a set of standard measures of a technology's cost-saving performance; and
- A mind set that thinks about technologies broadly, including their integration into other health care services and embedding of health care tools and data collection into the "Internet of things."

Again, she said, what is needed is a balance between the information needed now and the data that need to be collected to move home health care into the future.

QUESTIONS AND COMMENTS

An open discussion followed the panelists' presentations. Workshop participants were able to make comments and ask questions of the panelists. The following sections summarize the discussion session.

Design and Use of Technologies

Mary Brady, U.S. Food and Drug Administration (FDA), echoed the suggestion that one factor affecting whether technologies are actually used by people is how well they can be incorporated into the patient's life. Technologies that are too obtrusive are less acceptable, she said. One of the ways to find this out, she suggested, is through better human factors engineering and testing of the usability of a technology throughout the development process. Brady further noted that FDA has a guidance for industry related to premarket concerns.[2] She said that many types of technology that were not designed for nonclinical and home use are being used outside the clinical environment (where care is needed 24 hours per day, 7 days per week). The guidance asks industry to consider the design, the users, and the physical environment in which a device will be used.

Cindy Krafft, American Physical Therapy Association, said that some of the technologies in development have great potential to support patient

---

[2] See http://www.fda.gov/MedicalDevices/DeviceRegulationandGuidance/GuidanceDocuments/ucm331675.htm (accessed December 8, 2014).

functionality and activities of daily living. Still, she said, home health care agencies cannot make assumptions about their patients' ability to use the technology. Krafft gave the example of a case in which telehealth was used to report weight on a daily basis. However, she noted, home health care nurses need to be sure that patients can get on and off the scale by themselves; often, they cannot, which can lead to inaccurate data reporting.

Rehabilitation has been a great beneficiary of technological advances, Nilsen said, in part because technology can provide data between in-person visits. She gave as an example a program funded by the National Science Foundation in which physical therapists remotely gathered data from a Wii Balance Board.

Peter Boling, Virginia Commonwealth University, warned against the creation of technology silos, as has been done "with every other component of health care." He noted examples of the problems that silos engender, including delays in receiving monitoring data because of the way an information routing system is set up. He described a paraplegic patient who lay in bed for 3 days without food or water because he could not reach the phone and could not afford the $30 per month needed for a wearable alert device. Although Boling was confident that technologies can work, he said that they often fail because they are implemented to serve the developer's business model and not the needs of the population that could benefit. "The vision is out there, but the application is far behind," he said.

Incentives

Krafft noted that a tremendous opportunity exists to expand rehabilitation therapies to prevent patient decline and keep patients out of higher-cost care. Unfortunately, she said, the current payment methods discourage the widespread use of rehabilitation methods that might replace a reimbursable therapy visit. Demiris agreed that telehealth and similar technologies raise a concern that they will be used to replace actual visits. They could be a great convenience for patients and families, or they could result in a diminution of services. In the early days of telehealth, he said, advocates emphasized that these services would be an add-on (they would not replace visits), but later it became clear that, if that were true, they would not be cost-effective. Rather than visits lost or visits added, it is important to think about the effective coordination of the services needed to achieve agreed-upon outcomes. Technology is only one tool among many in service redesign, he said. Nilsen agreed, saying that rehabilitation technologies are often useful in providing data between in-person visits. At Almost Family, Inc., Kaushal said, physicians, nurses, and therapists focus on a plan of care instead of visits or technology. Each patient needs a plan of care that is integrated across clinical disciplines, that includes the appropriate technology, and that each discipline is following. "That is the biggest challenge we face in everyday life," he said.

Thomas E. Edes, U.S. Department of Veterans Affairs (VA), noted that in the VA's home-based primary care program, patients who receive 10 or more visits are recognized as having more complex conditions and are moved into a higher cost category. Of the 10 visits, half can be telehealth visits. To measure productivity within Almost Family, Inc., Kashaul said that the organization has developed an equivalency measure, in which some number of telehealth visits has been equated to one in-person visit. With this system (which is still being tested), staff who are paid per patient visit do not feel penalized for telehealth visits, he said. Kathryn H. Bowles, Visiting Nurse Service of New York Research Center and the University of Pennsylvania School of Nursing, said a further step would be to think about ways to reward clinicians who become more efficient. She described a randomized trial that she led in which the nurses were asked to replace some in-person visits with visits via the use of video technology. The trial found that nurses who were efficient could save time. They were then assigned additional patients, however, and so got more work. She said that one way to overcome that disincentive might be to base rewards on patient outcomes and counting telehealth encounters into the productivity standards rather than just the number of patient visits per day.

Evaluating New Technologies

Bruce Leff, Johns Hopkins University, questioned whether randomized controlled trials are really a robust method for evaluating these technologies. Technologies are not used in isolation, he said, but are used in the context of people, processes, and the planning of care. They are implemented in a very specific setting with a specific clinical team and social milieu. Moreover, trials take a long time and are very expensive. Leff noted that at present, Sarah Szanton is evaluating the CAPABLE program that she described (see Chapter 6) in two different ways: one way is through a classic trial funded by NIH in which she cannot change any of the protocol, and the other way is through the use of a challenge grant from the Center for Medicare & Medicaid Innovation, in which the evaluation is constantly being reinvented as it goes along.

Demiris acknowledged these challenges, adding that the technology itself may become outdated, given how long it takes to plan and carry out a randomized trial. Furthermore, technology does not operate independently of everything else. "So when you introduce, let's say, access to the Internet for a specific educational intervention," he said, "you can't prohibit patients from browsing other websites" that also may affect their behavior and you cannot prevent a wearable device that is being tested from being used for additional purposes. For these reasons, the use of "pragmatic clinical trials" or greater flexibility in the research protocol may be useful and allow the inevitable evolution of technology over the period of the research (Demiris, 2011).

Nilsen listed other kinds of trials—optimization trials, adaptive trials, and continuously evolving trials—that can be considered for the evaluation of technology. Moreover, ways to shorten the amount of time required for traditional randomized trials may exist. NIH is working on speeding up subject recruitment, for example, as well as shortening the time needed to obtain outcomes.

8

Making Connections

Earlier chapters addressed gaps and barriers in specific sectors of home health care (e.g., workforce, payment, models of care, technology). However, beyond these challenges, home health care sits within a larger system of care that needs to be considered. In one panel at the workshop, three speakers spoke about different connections that are needed to integrate home health care into the broader health care environment: connecting to the overall health care system, connecting to social services, and connecting data.

CONNECTING TO THE LARGER HEALTH CARE ECOSYSTEM

Barbara Gage
The Brookings Institution

Changes in the broader health ecosystem affect home health significantly, said Gage, especially as organizations focus on the triple aim of the Patient Protection and Affordable Care Act of 2010 (ACA)[1]: improving the patient experience of care (including quality and satisfaction), improving the health of populations, and reducing the per capita cost of health care. "These initiatives were always under way, but nobody had pulled them together into one related effort."

Gage reviewed a number of significant changes in the health care envi-

---

[1] Patient Protection and Affordable Care Act of 2010, Public Law 111-148, 111th Cong., 2nd sess. (March 23, 2010).

ronment that are in progress. She noted that the U.S. Congress has required that all Medicare-funded services have quality reporting programs in place, whereas in the past, only hospitals and nursing facilities had them. Innovative payment methods are focusing not only on the costs of care but also on outcomes, thus focusing the conversation—and payment—on value and not just ongoing payment for additional services. Shared savings from the achievement of quality goals are available to several categories of providers, and incentives to coordinate care are in place, she said. Finally, she said, accountable care organizations (ACOs) must integrate care across the health care system because they are financially responsible for patient outcomes.

Gage noted that additional new programs target specific populations, programs, and services, such as people who are eligible for both Medicare and Medicaid, programs of long-term services and supports (LTSS), and Medicaid efforts to serve more recipients in the community (rather than in nursing homes). The high-cost Medicare population and the population receiving LTSS tend to be the same people: those living in the community who have many medical and social support needs. "That's where home health really comes into the picture," she said. In addition, innovations, such as carve-out initiatives for high-risk populations, are occurring in the private payer sector.

Role of Home Health in the Medicare Program

Home health can play a number of central roles in this changing marketplace. Gage said that it can—and often does—provide the desired coordination across providers, whether it occurs at times of transition (e.g., from hospital to home) or between medical and social supports, and for patients and family caregivers it is often an educational resource describing care options and resources. Gage provided some data (MedPAC, 2013) about the people served in the Medicare home health program, showing that

- Sixty-six percent of patients enter a home health program from the community and not the hospital.
- Patients admitted from the community have an average of 3.8 chronic conditions, and 29 percent have Alzheimer's disease or dementia.
- Post-acute care patients have an average of 4.2 chronic conditions, and 21 percent of these patients have Alzheimer's disease or dementia.
- Forty-two percent of patients admitted from the community qualify for both Medicare and Medicaid, compared to 24 percent of post-acute care patients.

- Home health aide services represented the majority of services provided in 11 percent of the episodes for people admitted from the community, whereas they represented 4 percent of the services for post-acute care patients.

Every year, one in five Medicare beneficiaries is hospitalized, and about 35 percent of hospitalized individuals are discharged to post-acute care (Gage et al., 2009). Among the individuals in the population discharged to post-acute care, 38 percent use more than one post-acute care provider. About one-quarter of those who go to home health care are readmitted to the hospital. Some of these cases are medically complex and some are not, Gage said; some readmissions are avoidable and some are not.

Patients follow different paths after acute care, Gage noted. About 23 percent of those who go into a formal service program go directly to home health care and receive all the care that they need there (Gage et al., 2009). More complex patterns involve transitions from the hospital to a skilled nursing facility and then to home health care. About 8 percent follow this pattern, she said. Tracking these diverse pathways demonstrates that "when we talk about a person's services, it's really an episode," she said. "It isn't just one unique service."

Although some home health care patients have complex care needs, they probably do not need 24-hour nursing or they would have been discharged to a long-term care hospital, a rehabilitation hospital, or a skilled nursing facility, Gage said. On a scale from 1 to 100, home health patients have the highest mean self-care score, about 60, when they start home health care, she said, which is some 15 points higher than that for patients in skilled nursing facilities (Gage et al., 2012). Home health agencies also provide a large amount of therapy that is paid for by Medicare, but the level of care is much lower as compared to the level of therapy services provided to individuals in inpatient settings. Even so, Gage said, these therapy services may be keeping people mobile or able to carry out their activities of daily living (ADLs).

For outcomes, Gage's research shows that home health care is able to achieve a 10-point gain (about 15 percent) in patients' self-care functionality, which she calls "pretty impressive." If similar analyses comparing gains in self-care ability for similar groups of patients are done, home health care patients again have larger improvements than patients in other settings (Gage et al., 2012). Some of the accomplishments of home health care arise from the fact that it treats a somewhat different patient population, Gage said. It is especially helpful for patients with musculoskeletal problems, for example, but does not provide an advantage for patients with nervous system problems or strokes.

Role of Home Health in the Changing Health Care Marketplace

The nurse case managers who do initial home health assessments are automatically doing case management of the type endorsed in the newer models of the organization of care, Gage said. As health care reform reemphasizes person centeredness and focuses on care coordination, outcomes, and cost-effectiveness, home health gains in importance. Clinicians now need to follow patients "past their front door and into the community," Gage said, because now they are responsible for them 30, 60, or 90 days after hospital discharge, so what happens in the community is vitally important.

Home health agencies serve both the Medicare post-acute care and the LTSS populations. To the extent that hospitals are only just now learning about the need to take this longer-term, episode-based view, she said, they may not be as well integrated as desirable with the home health agencies in the community. In some locales, the home health agencies work closely with the agency on aging for that area, which can fill in additional pieces of the comprehensive care needs of a given patient. However, Gage said, there is a need for greater coordination, communication, and data standardization among service-providing agencies.

New legislation has directed the Centers for Medicare & Medicaid Services (CMS) to improve Medicare's post-acute care services and the reporting on them.[2] It will require home health agencies and other providers to submit data on quality measures, resource use, and standardized patient assessments. (It also includes a provision to study the effect of Medicare beneficiaries' "socioeconomic status on quality, resource use, and other measures" and the impact of specified risk factors on such measures.) This will result in a more national approach to quality measurement and to thinking about patients "in a consistent way," Gage said. Meanwhile, she said, there is consensus on how to measure key aspects of long-term care, like pressure ulcers, in ways that are reliable. Under the coordinated quality strategies of the U.S. Department of Health and Human Services, CMS is developing the infrastructure that will allow the electronic exchange of consensus-based quality measures that can be folded into bundled payments, for example. In many areas, she said, "standardized information is being moved into either the quality programs or the payment programs, or both."

The strengths of home health that Gage believes will help shape its future are the proven programs that home health agencies often provide, including both home health care and hospice; the broad array of services that they provide, including nursing, therapy, social work, and aide services;

---

[2] Improving Medicare Post-Acute Care Transformation (IMPACT) Act of 2014, Public Law 113-185, 113th Cong., 2nd sess. (October 6, 2014).

their placement in the community, where they know the local providers and often know the residents with more complex medical conditions; and the training of their staff in the coordination of services, such as medication reconciliation and social support, "which all of those different payment policy initiatives and quality metrics come back to: coordination and communication across the system." Gage believes that home health care is an underutilized resource, particularly as the health care environment moves toward managing patients across a continuum of care.

MEDICARING ACCOUNTABLE CARE COMMUNITIES: CONNECTING HEALTH CARE AND SOCIAL SERVICES

Anne Montgomery, Altarum Institute
Kyle Allen, Riverside Health Systems

The ultimate goal for the continuum of care, Montgomery said, would be "to connect acute care, post-acute care, community agencies, and LTSS." Although the U.S. Congress tried to establish such a program through the ACA, it was unsuccessful.[3] Because of this failure, she believes that this arena may not be revisited legislatively for "quite a while." Meanwhile, research and modeling that may reveal more viable approaches to making these connections "with existing programs, existing financing, and existing services" can continue.

Currently, because most health care policy is driven by budgetary and political considerations, policy skews strongly toward the status quo at a time when a lot of innovation and creativity is required, Montgomery said. At the Altarum Institute's Center for Elder Care and Advanced Illness, Joanne Lynn has continued to develop a locally anchored, comprehensive model called MediCaring accountable care communities (ACCs), which would create some of the needed connections, she said. The model, which would deliver both health care and LTSS, is tailored to address the needs of the rapidly growing population needing a broad spectrum of services, primarily people over age 65 years with two or more problems with ADLs, those with cognitive impairment needing constant supervision, and the oldest old (those age 85 years and older) who are medically frail and do not have much reserve. According to Montgomery, features of ACCs include

---

[3] The ACA included a Community Living Assistance Services and Supports (CLASS) Act, which would have instituted a voluntary, national, federally administered long-term care insurance program, but concerns about the program's projected high costs and likely difficulties with implementation and sustainability caused it to be repealed in 2013.

- Comprehensive longitudinal care plans that cover all settings where a person receives care, including the home, and that are grounded in patient preferences for treatment and quality-of-life goals;
- More efficient and appropriate medical care tailored to the often unique needs of frail elders that are not addressed by the current "sick care and episodic" model and made more readily accessible at home, including 24-hour on-call arrangements;
- The full range of health, social, and supportive services, including assessment of the adequacy of housing;
- Use of core funding derived from shared savings in a community ACO structure modified to serve the frail elderly population (MediCaring ACCs); and
- Ongoing monitoring and improvement guided locally by a community board that comprises providers, professional managers, community agencies, and stakeholders (e.g., employers, because of the net negative impact of caregiving on employee productivity, and health and local leaders), which anchors the project in the community and works toward achieving sustainability.

Building such care plans and convincing policy makers of their value would enable the kinds of documents that health and social service providers could more easily follow on the basis of an understanding of "which services work, which are cost-effective, which are timely, and when they need to be adjusted," Montgomery said. "The longitudinal care plan is sort of like the trunk of a tree, where all the treating providers are branches off of it." Such plans are likely to be more administratively efficient as well, she said, because they would constitute a single plan and not the cumbersome and time-consuming multiple plans developed by different providers today in a "sick care/episodic care" delivery model. In aggregate, such care plans could aid with estimations of the need for services and workforce capacity in a given locale and whether too many or too few workers are available for the number of elders needing services.

Allen has been working on a project funded through the ACA's Community-Based Care Transitions Program[4] in two communities across the country and has been struck by the infrastructure built through the Administration on Aging Services in these communities. One of these projects worked with five local area agencies on aging as part of the Eastern Virginia Care Transitions Partnership, which covers about 7,500 square miles and both rural and urban areas. The partnership involves 11 hospitals in 5 different health care systems and is enrolling 900 people per month in a community-based care transitions model. In addition, Allen worked with

---

[4] See http://innovation.cms.gov/initiatives/CCTP (accessed December 30, 2014).

Altarum to design a Center for Medicare & Medicaid Innovation grant proposal tailored to four communities: Akron, Ohio; Milwaukie, Oregon; Queens, New York; and Williamsburg, Virginia.

These MediCaring ACCs, which are still in the development phase, would coordinate funding from multiple payers—Medicare and Medicaid, the Older Americans Act, state and local programs, and private sources—and in the process wring out current waste and inappropriate services and then reinvest and redeploy some of that funding for social services or to improve housing. The United States is quite different from the rest of the developed nations in the share of aggregate social services spending that goes to these health-related supports, which is very low, she said.

A package of waivers of existing Medicare rules would be necessary to pilot test the MediCaring ACC program, Montgomery said, among which are

- Waiving the Medicare rule limiting skilled nursing or therapy services delivery in the home to those who are homebound,
- Allowing nurse practitioners to authorize home health care or hospice services in states where that is permitted, and
- Allowing ACOs or other entities to enroll only frail elders and allow the geographic concentration of services.

The most important waiver is the last one, she said, which would allow shared savings across the bundle of services for this population.

Allen said that he is confident that this model could be funded through the projected savings that it will generate. A detailed financial model has been developed for four communities with extremely varied health care systems.

CONNECTING THE DATA

Terrence O'Malley
Massachusetts General Hospital

O'Malley harked back to the story related by James Martinez (see Chapter 1, Box 1-2), saying that individuals and their caregivers are the heart of the system. Swirling around them are all the other services that they need, he said, including health and wellness services, medical care, social services, LTSS, and home health care. Creating a new care model will depend on increasing the connections among them. "In health care, we're a bunch of silos," he said. "We only connect around the exchange of information around a patient, but the issue is what happens between the silos. It's the white space."

O'Malley reflected on previous presentations, noting that home health care alone offers a wide range of services, from hospital-in-the-home types of practices to the services of a person who can make home repairs. New standards and processes are critical to managing the array of services needed by people with multiple chronic conditions, disabilities, and frailty, he said. Innovative care models are having dramatic results in targeting high-risk patients, and O'Malley believes that these models are scalable. To bridge the gap between the current service delivery silos, O'Malley said that it will be necessary to add more social services to the medical model or more medical services to the social services model or develop ways to integrate them. Additional challenges include the need to make the transitions between sites of care or between different teams that provide care safe, close the open loops in referral management, and coordinate care across an entire episode (longitudinally), and engage providers so that they are working off the same patient care plan. Home health agencies could potentially be the manager or integrator of all these services, he said.

Although communication is vitally important in the creation of a coordinated system, home health and LTSS programs are unlikely to be able to afford costly electronic health records systems, O'Malley said. Numerous workshop participants pointed out that their home health agency used a data system different from the ones used by other providers in their networks. According to O'Malley, the creation of a shared information platform is therefore a significant challenge that will require the following:

- A compelling business case,
- The use of health information exchanges or other exchange mechanisms to connect with others,
- Low-cost ways to access the exchanges,
- Adoption of common data management standards to transmit data reliably,
- Standardized information that is meaningful to providers and others who can use it to monitor system performance, and
- Effective channels for two-way communication between service providers and patients and families.

O'Malley said that the information platform for home health needs to be inexpensive, easy to use, and reliable—"standardized and interoperable," in the words of the Office of the National Coordinator for Health Information Technology (ONCHIT). ONCHIT has selected a standard for patient information exchange called the consolidated data architecture (CDA), and a library of reusable data templates that can be combined to form CDA documents exists. These documents can be of any size but use a specific syntax. "It's just like Legos," he said, noting that the different pieces can come in many varieties but that they all work together and can be packaged in different ways.

As an example, O'Malley cited a project in Worcester, Massachusetts, in which the electronic record begins being built when the patient enters the emergency room and continues to be built through admission, is added to during the hospital stay, and upon discharge is sent to the skilled nursing facility (via low-cost, Web-based software called a surrogate electronic environment [SEE]). The information that the nursing facility collects for the Long-Term Care Minimum Data Set (MDS)[5] is added to the CDA file and reconsolidated by SEE. Upon discharge from the nursing facility, an updated document is sent to home health and the primary care physician. What they learned in working on this project, O'Malley said, was not that they needed hundreds of different data sets, as was initially feared, but that by using the CDA system, they needed only five:

1. The test or procedure report—what the clinician needs to get back when ordering a test;
2. The test or procedure request—what the clinician needs to send when ordering the test;
3. The shared care encounter summary—what the clinician needs to get back from a consultant (whether it is a specialist physician or the emergency department);
4. The consultation request clinical summary—what the clinician needs to send to a consultant; and
5. The transfer of care summary—what the institution needs to send when there is a permanent transfer of care (a discharge to any other site).

Every care site that receives a patient needs surprisingly similar information, O'Malley said. The data sets (described above) are nested, and many of the data elements in the smaller sets are reused in the larger sets. This is possible because the data elements are all interoperable and standardized.

The home health and longitudinal plans of care include many data elements that would already exist in these transitions of care data sets, plus some additional elements, O'Malley said. The plans of care are based on medical, surgical, nursing, behavioral, cognitive, and psychological issues, as well as information about function and the environment (e.g., housing,

---

[5] The MDS "is a standardized, primary screening and assessment tool of health status that forms the foundation of the comprehensive assessment for all residents in a Medicare and/or Medicaid-certified long-term care facility. The MDS contains items that measure physical, psychological and psychosocial functioning" (CMS, 2012).

supports, transportation). These can be mapped to the data sets. Specific medical conditions or medication-based expansions can be included. "If you can exchange not so much the care plan but the interoperable, critical parts of a plan—concerns, interventions, goals, and assigned team members—the receivers can reuse those components in their own care planning process," he said. According to O'Malley, the components of a CDA document can include the following, among many other elements:

- Patient history and physical notes,
- Progress notes,
- Diagnostic imaging reports,
- Operative notes,
- Procedure notes,
- A discharge summary,
- A continuity-of-care document,
- Consultation notes,
- Referral notes,
- A transfer summary, and
- A care plan.

Each of these sections can be broken down into multiple fields of information.

Again, he said, building this will require shared mechanisms to exchange health information and the acquisition and use of low-cost software. Once the CDAs are created, they can be used for additional purposes, such as reporting on quality and management of population health. This model represents a solution to the challenge of sharing essential health information across different sites to facilitate the level of care coordination needed by patients with complex medical conditions, O'Malley said.

If home health agencies participate in this shared information exchange between health care and community-based service providers, it provides them with the opportunity to play a number of new roles, in addition to the role of service provider, O'Malley said. "This gets home care away from merely selling the commodity of home care visits." Home health agencies can become aggregators, integrators, managers, and guarantors of the range of services needed by individuals with complex health care needs. In so doing, he said, they can sell value, which comes with the integration of services and with the establishment of these services as reliable, consistent, and scalable. "The reason home care can do this," O'Malley said, "is that no one else in the health sector does—or can do—what home care does, by bringing services to the individual, not the other way around, by providing services in geographically dispersed areas, not a fixed location, and by being the bridge between traditional health care and community-based service providers."

QUESTIONS AND COMMENTS

A brief open discussion followed the panelists' presentations. Workshop participants were able to give comments and ask questions of the panelists. The following sections summarize the discussion session.

Montgomery noted that the Improving Medicare Post-Acute Care Transformation (IMPACT) Act of 2014[6] will require reporting on standardized measures that will give a much closer look at patient function and a broader view of service provider capabilities, as well as greater accountability across post-acute care settings.[7] Gage said that the act's quality metrics are all basic information that home health agencies already monitor and collect.

Even with more standardized post-acute care metrics, coordination of these services with hospitals is likely to continue to pose challenges. Peter Boling, Virginia Commonwealth University, related a story about one of his patients and said that even having an electronic health record that notes the identity of a patient's primary care physician does not prevent assignment to another doctor for follow-up if the patient ends up in the hospital of a different health care system. Patients need a greater say in which hospital and system that they are taken to, O'Malley said. In addition, basic rules of the road will have to be worked out between health care providers and shared savings plans, which are accountable for the full care of a patient, whether that is delivered in network or by others, he said. Obviously, plans would prefer to have their patients under their supervision and care. Allen added that patient education in advance about the importance of staying in the correct managed care model (or, in his experience, Program of All-Inclusive Care for the Elderly [PACE]) to avoid out-of-pocket costs may be a partial approach. In addition, O'Malley said, the emergency medical technicians who take the patient to the out-of-network hospital also should be part of

---

[6] Improving Medicare Post Acute Care Transformation Act of 2014, Public Law 113-185, 113th Cong., 2nd sess. (October 6, 2014).

[7] According to Montgomery, under the IMPACT Act, the new quality measures that all post-acute care providers will be required to report are "functional status, cognitive function, and special services; treatments and interventions, such as the need for ventilator use, dialysis, chemotherapy, central line placement, and total parenteral nutrition; medical conditions and comorbidities, such as diabetes, congestive heart failure, and pressure ulcers; impairments such as incontinence and impaired ability to hear, see, or swallow; and other categories deemed necessary and appropriate by the Secretary."

the information exchange. They should be able to download all the information that they need about the patient, including hospital preference, he said. Part of the organization around MediCaring ACCs involves bringing the emergency medical service providers to the table, Allen noted. Just by working more closely together locally, improvements in how services are linked can be made. On the West Coast, an increasing number of emergency services programs are actually functioning like case managers, because they know the patients who return often to the hospitals, Gage said. "They know the home; they know where the patient needs to go."

9

Reflections and Reactions

At the beginning of the second day of the workshop, two of the moderators for panels presented on the first day of the workshop reflected on the key messages they heard regarding what it will take to get to the ideal state of home health care. These included the panels that addressed workforce considerations and new organizational and payment models.[1] Then, in the final session of the workshop, three individuals presented their reactions to the workshop overall. Some of the recurrent topics identified by these individuals are highlighted in Box 9-1.

The following sections are the reflections and reactions of the members of these two panels.

REFLECTIONS ON DAY ONE

This section summarizes the reflections of moderators for panels on workforce (see Chapter 5) and models of care and approaches to payment (see Chapter 6) presented on the first day of the workshop.

---

[1] For personal reasons, Barbara B. Citarella was unable to present her reflections for the panel on key issues and trends (see Chapter 4).

BOX 9-1
Highlights from Individual Speakers

The following are topics identified by individual reactors as being recurrent topics from the workshop's presentations:

- A focus on the sickest, highest-cost patients (Bowles, Lee)
- The need for quality and outcomes measurement (Labson, Lee)
- The potential for cost savings (Bowles, Lee)
- The need for better transitions of care and better coordination of care (Bowles, Labson, Lee, Stein)
- The appropriate use of technology, including information technology and telehealth (Bowles, Labson, Lee, Stein, Taler)
- Support for family caregivers (Bowles, Labson)
- Improved training for and use of the home health care workforce (Bowles, Labson, Taler)
- The need to focus on an individual's level of function (Bowles, Labson, Lee, Taler)
- The need for flexible payment approaches (Bowles, Lee)
- The need for patient-centered goal setting (Lee, Stein)
- The need for better connections between health care and social services (Stein, Taler)

Workforce

Margherita C. Labson
The Joint Commission

Among the points emphasized in the workforce panel, Labson said, was the compelling need for robust methods of analysis of workforce topics. Thomas E. Edes, in particular, she said, demonstrated how helpful information can be in program development. Targeting of high-risk, high-cost, and vulnerable populations for home-based primary care unquestionably requires a more diverse and skilled workforce, and his data showed "how much better it is to approach these clients at the primary care phase rather than waiting until they need restorative care," Labson said. In addition to targeting, which all panelists emphasized, Edes discussed the needs for strong transition programs. Labson pointed out that these junctures in the health care continuum are places where the risk of error is highest.

The U.S. Department of Veterans Affairs (VA) has the advantage of having a system-wide electronic record system, a capacity that is "woefully lacking in the industry at large," Labson said. However, several other presenters during the day mentioned that although many of the delivery systems may have a single record, their hospice or home health care services do not, at least not yet.

As noted by Gail Hunt, the willingness as well as the ability of family caregivers to provide home health care is important to a successful home care situation, Labson said. Caregiving responsibilities change people's lives, and some of these changes lead to better organization. This is perhaps a lesson implicit in health professionals' training of family members for more specific caregiving tasks. Like Edes, Hunt pointed to the appropriate use of technology in the home, Labson noted, and she emphasized the importance of using patient-reported outcomes as one of the measures of effectiveness of a program.

Robyn I. Stone described some of the different types of health workers in the direct care workforce, with each one having somewhat different, but sometimes overlapping, responsibilities and capacities. According to Labson, Stone provided a realistic appraisal of the future of the direct care worker, which will be affected by the

- shrinking availability of family caregivers,
- changing demographics of direct care workers and their patients,
- availability of career lattices that allow ongoing career development,
- low wages and scant benefits, and
- overall health of the U.S. economy.

Improvements in the performance of this workforce will require improvements in competency-based training, supervision, worker empowerment, wages and benefits, and the potential for career advancement in specialty areas, such as comorbidity care or dementia care, Labson said.

According to Labson, the independence at home and consumer-directed care movements were touchstones for the remarks of Henry Claypool. He emphasized the value of *promotora*-type care, as opposed to rehabilitative care, for people in their homes and the need for those with clinical training to empower their clients. Rather than a narrow focus on clinical issues, he supported the broader attention to functional issues. With respect to direct care workers, the skilled/unskilled dichotomy is pejorative and may inhibit direct care workers from taking their appropriate place on the interdisciplinary team, Labson said.

Models of Care and Approaches to Payment

Teresa L. Lee
Alliance for Home Health Quality and Innovation

Key themes from the panel, which included the overview by Peter Boling and descriptions of six diverse programs, were presented by Teresa L. Lee. She noted that most of the discussion focused on the very sickest, highest-cost patients, defined by the use of different definitions for classifying such individuals by different programs. These patients were described as having multiple chronic conditions and functional limitations; being treated with multiple (sometimes conflicting) medications for multiple conditions; and being frequent users of hospitals, emergency departments, and nursing homes. To identify these patients, Lee noted, most of the models use various types of risk stratification, which requires health information systems sufficient to perform such stratifications, adequate patient assessment protocols, and data analytics.

Lee said the diverse care delivery and payment models described encompassed everything from advanced illness management to bundled payment arrangements, accountable care organizations, home-based primary care, and hospital at home, all with home health or home-based care components. Despite this variation, Lee noted a number of common elements among the home health care models discussed:

- Home health care services are integrated with primary care, specifically physicians and advanced practice nurses, and palliative and end-of-life care programs.
- Home health care services focus on care coordination, care management, and care transitions.
- Most models include post-acute care, and all models are working toward proactive, preventive maintenance care.
- Nursing care and physical or occupational therapy play critical roles, and in some models, the role of home health aides is being strengthened.
- The models use telehealth and remote monitoring (even low-tech approaches) to engage patients and increase program efficiency.

Person-centered goal setting and the integration of family caregivers into care teams were also important themes raised by panelists, Lee said. In particular, the Community Aging in Place—Advancing Better Living for Elders (CAPABLE) model presented by Sarah L. Szanton emphasized the use of the priorities of each individual receiving care to establish goals for that person. These goals may not be related to health or medical goals or needs, Lee said.

Lee further noted that although a number of the models that were described are emerging, some already have data on their impact on quality and cost outcomes over different time frames, although they include different populations and use different evaluation methods. Nevertheless, the patterns in the data were similar, showing dramatic reductions in hospitalization rates; the numbers of rehospitalizations, emergency department visits, and days in intensive care units (ICUs); and total costs per enrollee.

According to Lee, the policy and payment reforms that would strengthen these models and allow their expansion included the following: appropriate reimbursement for services geared to the stabilization or improvement of patients' functional status; approaches to the use of bundled payments for post-acute care that allow more flexibility in the delivery of care through the use of a waiver of the Medicare requirement that patients be home-bound and improved coordination with primary care; encouragement of the use of capitation, which also facilitates flexible payment approaches; and the use of value-based purchasing.

The vertical integration of a number of the models has led to the alignment of incentives by payers and providers, enabled a consensus on a financial bottom line, and improved communication among payers and providers, Lee said. For programs operating on a smaller scale, panelists recommended that a focus be placed on best practices, protocols for the tracking of quality and costs metrics, and the avoidance of expansion faster than the program can deliver positive results.

Finally, Lee raised the unasked question about the extent to which the new models are able to improve rates of diagnosis of certain specific diseases or conditions (e.g., dementia) and ultimately reduce preventable hospitalizations.

FINAL REACTORS PANEL

This section presents the remarks of three individuals who reflected on the workshop presentations overall, including their individual thoughts on themes that they heard throughout the 2 days of the workshop. In addition, after these formal remarks were provided, several workshop participants contributed some final thoughts.

Kathryn H. Bowles
Visiting Nurse Service of New York Research Center and University of Pennsylvania School of Nursing

In summarizing what she considered to be the main themes during the 2 days of the workshop, Bowles began by emphasizing the opportunity to shift care from costly acute and institutional care to the home and community. She noted many examples showing that home health care costs less. She found the frequent emphasis on patient function to be well received, including the need for exercise, physical therapy, and other interventions attempting to support patient function.

Bowles thought that Steven Landers's key ingredients needed repetition: the use of physician- and nurse practitioner (NP)-led holistic care plans, an enhanced capacity for an acute care response, thoughtful use of information technology to fill gaps and to communicate, and enhanced support during transitions. She also reiterated his message that home health "must rise to the occasion and embrace value creation."

Bowles indicated that speakers also emphasized the importance of the provision of care by interdisciplinary teams and occasionally mentioned the importance of including the patient and family caregiver as part of the team. Bowles noted that it is important to consider the home health and personal aide workforce to be members of the team, especially in their role as the eyes and ears for other team members.

The movement toward team-based care suggests the need for somewhat different training in medical and nursing schools and in other health professions schools, she said. "We need to be in class together, in the clinic together; we need to be problem solving together from the beginning." Training programs need to add content about the role of home- and community-based care and the excitement that can come from that type of care, she said. Home health care providers also need continuing education and updating of their training and tools. Bowles also noted the need to improve the efficiency of the processes within home health care, including intake procedures, prioritization of new cases, and the frequency of home visits.

Further, Bowles said, care should appear to be seamless to patients and providers, but hard work will be required to make that happen. Information technology can increase opportunities to communicate, share information, monitor patients, teach, support the work, and evaluate outcomes. These information systems need patient portals that allow information gathering and sharing and that improve self-care. The VA's information system can be examined for lessons, she added.

Standards facilitate the ability to share information across systems. Bowles noted that the American Nurses Association recognized a standardized, point-of-care terminology, the Omaha System for documenting in-home care and other care in four domains: environmental, psychosocial, physiological, and health-related behavior.[2] Multidisciplinary clinicians use that system to document problems, record signs and symptoms related to

---

[2] For more information, see http://www.omahasystem.org/overview.html (accessed December 9, 2014).

those problems and their interventions, and rate outcomes, she said. In 2014, Minnesota approved a statewide electronic health record and data exchange initiative and recommended that the Omaha System be one of the standards used. Such standardized data will help with the identification of best practices and the development of evidence-based protocols, Bowles suggested.

According to Bowles, a number of barriers to the greater use of technology needs attention. The lack of multistate professional licensure and restrictions on NPs inhibit their ability to practice at the top of their license; another is the integration of telehealth and other technologies into daily work. For such integration to happen, Bowles said, technologies must be easy to use and produce timelier results, and telehome alerts need to be smarter and produce fewer false alarms. Technologies are needed that support medication administration, reconciliation, and reminders; that send information to clinicians, including decision support, at the point of care; that can take on some of the inefficient, repetitive teaching in home health care; and that can provide support through the use of social networks. Although telehealth may be a useful tool for the field, she said, much more needs to be learned about it so that it may be used effectively and efficiently.

Identification of the right levels of care for patients coming out of the acute care setting is still not easy, Bowles said, particularly because discharge planning is not standardized. Patients not infrequently refuse post-acute care services because they do not understand their importance. Another need is to increase support for people to age in place and to help them focus on their goals and the care outcomes important to them.

"Our greatest barrier," Bowles said, "remains the payment models." The following were some of the ideas from the workshop that she noted were more thought-provoking:

- The emphasis on the most costly 5 (or 10) percent (What about everyone else, she asked?);
- The suggestion that the number of chronic illnesses is less important than the effects of the chronic illnesses on patient function;
- Reconceptualization of community care as pre-acute care and a focus on keeping people healthy and out of the hospital rather than the reverse; and
- The VA's medical foster home program as an innovative concept.

Judith Stein
Center for Medicare Advocacy

Stein, as an advocate for Medicare beneficiaries having difficulties with the current health care system, pointed to several presenters' emphasis on patient priorities, agreeing that people want to set their own goals and priorities and that "priorities" may be a better word for this than "goals." She said, "I don't think I've ever heard, when I've spoken with the people I was trying to get services from, 'Well, what does the patient want?'" She went on to emphasize a number of themes.

Many workshop presenters discussed the provision of as much patient support as possible in the community, she said, which means that the location for the provision of care is not limited to the patient's home. She believes that more discussion of collateral issues like transportation and housing is needed. The intervention from individuals who can help make repairs around the home was welcome, she said, because in her experience, simple issues prevent people from being able to stay in their homes, for example, needing a safety bar for the bathtub or a ramp to get up to the porch.

Coordinated care was another theme that Stein identified. Coordination of all aspects of an individual's care, including skilled, medical, and nonskilled services, is key to successful outcomes, she said. She expressed concern, however, that although Medicare Advantage strives to manage the costs of care, it has not proven to be able to coordinate care. Coordination of care means to "coordinate the services, the transportation, the housing, the physicians," she said. "[It] does not mean to 'manage the dollars, save the dollars.'"

Although the need for a willing and available caregiver received attention, "a willing and available patient" is also needed, Stein said. People sometimes refuse services because they do not understand them or the need for them, as was mentioned regarding post-acute care. "How you communicate is incredibly important," she said, and there also needs to be sensitivity to what individuals are comfortable with. For example, mothers do not necessarily want their daughters or sons to tend to their bathroom needs, she explained.

The workshop participants were rightfully focused on what technology can mean, she believes. However, she noted that at the Center for Medicare Advocacy, staff members have encountered denial after denial of Medicare claims for durable medical equipment, prosthetic devices, and speech-generating devices. The implication, she said, is that creative uses of technology that are most useful to beneficiaries may run afoul of coverage rules. This is short-sighted and counterproductive for beneficiaries, providers, and the Medicare program, Stein said.

The interpretation of Medicare rules that limits home health care to post-acute care situations remains a serious problem, despite the *Jimmo v. Sebelius* decision, Stein said. For these and other reasons, she said, "we need a 21st century Medicare program" that addresses contemporary patient and caregiver needs and considers medical and technological advances.

George Taler
MedStar Washington Hospital Center and
Georgetown University School of Medicine

All aspects of the U.S. health care system have been based on the medical model, focused on the illnesses and disabilities of the individual, and "we need to move it much more towards an emphasis on healthy communities," said Taler. He cited the conceptual shift, suggested by speaker Wendy J. Nilsen, from the consideration of home health care as health care in the home to consideration of the home as a place to be healthy and safe and was the central locus of care.

He sees care in the home to be a proverbial three-legged stool, supported by health care, social services, and function. In his model, health care is not about a set of consultative clinicians and supporting professionals; it is about an interdisciplinary team working for a population "to whom they are responsible personally and accountable to society." The social work leg of the stool should involve not just the brokering and pulling together of services, as they are now mostly used, but also counseling of patients and family caregivers and provision of a community organization function, he said, enjoining family, friends, and local agencies, such as the neighborhood village movement. Housing and function work together, are intimately related, and either limit or facilitate what can be accomplished in the home. By enlisting the help of neighbors and volunteers and with the aid of small grants and donations, older adults can age in place, which promotes age-related diversity in the community and maintains property values that benefit all.

Taler then suggested that the workshop participants conduct a thought experiment. He asked them to envision a matrix. Down the left margin, they should list functions (activities of daily living, instrumental activities of daily living, patient goals, and so on). The next columns are used to answer a series of questions from left to right:

- What is the patient's current status? Which of those activities and goals are they able to accomplish (determined by the use of whatever assessment scale is convenient)?
- Where is the patient likely to go, relative to those activities and goals, with the help of medical care, devices, rehabilitation services, and so on, including patient motivation?
- What is the caregiver willing and able do to fill in the gaps?
- What can the formal care system do to train the caregiver, provide additional assistance, or provide devices to fill in the gaps a little better?
- What can secondary caregivers—neighbors, friends, relatives, or paid assistance—contribute?

This exercise begins to create a care plan that focuses squarely on function and sets priorities, he suggested.

Taler endorsed speaker Robyn I. Stone's emphasis on the importance of direct care workers as part of the home health care team. They need adequate training and a care plan that helps them know what they need to do, how to be effective eyes and ears for the team, and how to be accountable not only to the team but also for their contribution to the outcomes of their patients, he said.

Meanwhile, he noted, the country faces a dearth of geriatricians. The geriatric NPs have been folded in with the adult NPs, and only a handful of physical therapists with geriatric expertise exist. The future workforce, Taler said, is a serious concern. The chronic care management field needs primary care physicians who are truly engaged in "the intellectual challenges of managing the complexity of [the medical conditions of] these patients, not only because of the joys of working in an interdisciplinary team but also for the emotional satisfaction of dealing with people at this time in their lives." Remunerative positions will be needed to attract these physicians, and the funds will likely come from shared savings programs under development through Medicare.

Taler also noted that much attention was given to technology issues, including monitoring technologies. Not discussed, he said, were practice management technologies that optimize clinicians' time, facilitate communication, and utilize point-of-service diagnostic technologies that permit informed decisions to be made on the fly, in patients' homes. "With about 20 pounds of equipment costing perhaps $20,000, it is possible to do in the home anything that an urgent care center can do," he said. Going further, he said that with the right financial incentives, within 4 hours it is possible to create a nursing home, hospital, or intensive care unit in a patient's bedroom. "There's no need to go to a hospital for the vast majority of problems, except major surgery, invasive procedures, and complex imaging." Preoperative and postoperative care can be done at home with ICU-level monitoring devices wirelessly connecting to a central telemetry unit. Taler also noted the lack of discussion about the specific technologies that can facilitate home-delivered medications and treatments.

Taler stated that neither hospitals nor primary care (as it is currently structured) can handle the wave of older patients requiring care for chronic conditions. He also said that current home health care organizations are unsustainable, but no one wants to be in a nursing home. For that reason, Taler challenged innovative home health care leaders to stop thinking about themselves as small fish in a large pond and instead "think about us as oxygen in the tank. If we don't succeed, our health care system dies."

FINAL THOUGHTS FROM WORKSHOP PARTICIPANTS

Amy Berman, The John A. Hartford Foundation, said the current system has many incentives to move in directions that would preclude home health care. When the future is considered, the health care system has a tremendous regulatory burden with respect to what is accomplished in that first home health visit. As a result, she said, home health providers are not necessarily focused on accomplishing what is of the greatest importance to patients until the second, third, or fourth visit. This includes the provision of assistance to the family to help them understand how to handle different aspects of care.

Berman also noted that for many people, caregiving is managed at a distance; that is, children do not necessarily live close to their parents any longer. Information sharing—and the Health Insurance Portability and Accountability Act[3]—should not be a barrier to this, even though, at present, it often is cited as being a barrier to team-based dialog.

Karen Marshall, Kadamba Tree Foundation, noted that people often come to the issue of care at home in a moment of crisis. People need a bridge between the present and future, she said, so that they have realistic expectations of what it means to have a long-term illness and to age. Some education could take place in the long period of time that exists before a crisis.

Michael Johnson, BAYADA Home Health Care, said that professionals should be interested not in what they are teaching patients and caregivers but in what they are learning. "We continue to talk about teaching, he said, and I just want to be sure that we're talking about learning, and how we measure that."

For the delivery of high-level, high-quality care at home, Anthony Sung described a pioneering project at Duke University: home-based bone marrow transplantation. Although this is one of the most advanced technical medical procedures, the Duke team has successfully treated seven patients in home-based settings. Sung argued that it is better for patients in terms of improved quality of life and decreased exposures to infection, and the clinicians believe that it also will improve other outcomes. Home health care preserves patients' normal microflora, he said, and in that way can improve homeostasis and health.

The workshop concluded with a final comment from Judith Stein: "I just want to say, we should unite. We have nothing to lose but our silos."

---

[3] Health Insurance Portability and Accountability Act of 1996, Public Law 104-191, 104th Cong., 2nd sess. (August 21, 1996).

References

Beales, J. L., and T. Edes. 2009. Veteran's Affairs Home Based Primary Care. *Clinics in Geriatric Medicine* 25(1):149–154.

CMS (Centers for Medicare & Medicaid Services). 2012. *Long-Term Care Minimum Data Set.* http://www.cms.gov/Research-Statistics-Data-and-Systems/Files-for-Order/Identifiable DataFiles/LongTermCareMinimumDataSetMDS.html (accessed January 22, 2015).

CMS. 2014. *Jimmo v. Sebelius settlement agreement: Fact sheet.* http://www.cms.gov/Medicare/ Medicare-Fee-for-Service-Payment/SNFPPS/Downloads/Jimmo-FactSheet.pdf (accessed December 30, 2014).

Coleman, E. A., C. Parry, S. Chalmers, and S. J. Min. 2006. The care transitions intervention: Results of a randomized controlled trial. *Archives of Internal Medicine* 166(17): 1822–1828.

Counsell, S. R., C. M. Callahan, D. O. Clark, W. Tu, A. B. Buttar, T. E. Stump, and G. D. Ricketts. 2007. Geriatric care management for low-income seniors: A randomized controlled trial. *Journal of the American Medical Association* 298(22):2623–2633.

De Jonge, K. E., N. Jamshed, D. Gilden, J. Kubisiak, S. R. Broce, and G. Taler. 2014. Effects of home-based primary care on Medicare costs in high-risk elders. *Journal of the American Geriatrics Society* 62(10):1825–1831.

Demiris, N. A. 2011. A pragmatic view on pragmatic trials. *Dialogues in Clinical Neuroscience* 13(2):217–224.

Edes, T., B. Kinosian, N. H. Vuckovic, L. O. Nichols, M. M. Becker, and M. Hossain. 2014. Better access, quality, and cost for clinically complex veterans with home-based primary care. *Journal of the American Geriatrics Society* 62(10):1954–1961.

Gage, B., M. Morley, P. Spain, and M. Ingber. 2009. *Examining post acute care relationships in an integrated hospital system.* Waltham, MA: RTI International.

Gage, B., M. Morley, L. Smith, M. J. Ingber, A. Deutsch, T. Kline, J. Dever, J. Abbate, R. Miller, B. Lyda-McDonald, C. Kelleher, D. Garfinkel, J. Manning, C. M. Murtaugh, M. Stineman, and T. Mallinson. 2012. *Post-acute care payment reform demonstration: Final report.* Research Triangle Park, NC: RTI International.

IOM (Institute of Medicine). 2008. *Retooling for an aging America: Building the health care workforce.* Washington, DC: The National Academies Press.

Kaiser Family Foundation. 2014. *Medicare at a glance.* http://kff.org/medicare/fact-sheet/medicare-at-a-glance-fact-sheet (accessed December 31, 2014).

Leff, B., L. Burton, S. L. Mader, B. Naughton, J. Burl, S. K. Inouye, W. B. Greenough III, S. Guido, C. Langston, K. D. Frick, D. Steinwachs, and J. R. Burton. 2005. Hospital at home: Feasibility and outcomes of a program to provide hospital-level care at home for acutely ill older patients. *Annals of Internal Medicine* 143(11):798–808.

MedPAC (Medicare Payment Advisory Commission). 2013. *Report to the Congress: Medicare payment policy.* Washington, DC: MedPAC.

Naylor, M. D., D. Brooten, R. Campbell, B. S. Jacobsen, M. D. Mezey, M. V. Pauly, and J. S. Schwartz. 1999. Comprehensive discharge planning and home follow-up of hospitalized elders: A randomized clinical trial. *Journal of the American Medical Association* 281(7):613–620.

NRC (National Research Council). 2011. *Health care comes home: The human factors.* Washington, DC: The National Academies Press.

Rural Assistance Center. 2015. *Promotora de salud/lay health worker model.* http://www.raconline.org/communityhealth/chw/module2/layhealth (accessed January 23, 2015).

RWJF (Robert Wood Johnson Foundation). 2013. *Cash & counseling.* http://www.rwjf.org/en/research-publications/find-rwjf-research/2013/06/cash---counseling.html (accessed January 23, 2015).

Shaughnessy, P. W., D. R. Hittle, K. S. Crisler, M. C. Powell, A. A. Richard, A. M. Kramer, R. E. Schlenker, J. F. Steiner, N. S. Donelan-McCall, J. M. Beaudry, K. L. Mulvey-Lawlor, and K. Engle. 2002. Improving patient outcomes of home health care: Findings from two demonstration trials of outcome-based quality improvement. *Journal of the American Geriatrics Society* 50(8):1354–1364.

Wieland, D., R. Boland, J. Baskins, and B. Kinosian. 2010. Five-year survival in a program of all-inclusive care for elderly compared with alternative institutional and home- and community-based care. *The Journals of Gerontology, Series A: Biological Sciences and Medical Sciences* 65(7):721–726.

Appendix A

Workshop Agenda

The Future of Home Health Care: A Workshop

September 30–October 1, 2014

The Keck Center of the National Academies
500 Fifth Street, NW, Room 100
Washington, DC 20001

Sponsored by:

Alliance for Home Health Quality and Innovation
American Academy of Home Care Medicine
American Nurses Association
American Physical Therapy Association
Axxess
Community Health Accreditation Program
Home Instead Senior Care
National Alliance for Caregiving
Unity Point at Home

Workshop Objectives

- Provide an overview of the current state of home health care.
- Examine the particular role of Medicare-certified home health agencies in achieving the triple aim: to improve the quality of patient care, improve population health, and reduce costs.
- Explore how to integrate home health care into the future health care marketplace.
- Discuss how to facilitate the future role of home health care (e.g., workforce, technology, infrastructure, policy reform).
- Highlight research priorities to help clarify the value of home health care.

DAY ONE: September 30, 2014

8:45 a.m.	**Welcome and Remarks on the Ecosystem of Home Health**

Bruce Leff, *Workshop Co-Chair*
Johns Hopkins University School of Medicine

Elizabeth Madigan, *Workshop Co-Chair*
Case Western Reserve University

CONSUMER PERSPECTIVE

9:15 a.m.   James Martinez

KEYNOTE: HOME HEALTH CARE—THE CURRENT STATE

9:30 a.m.   Robert J. Rosati
Visiting Nurse Association (VNA) Health Group

9:55 a.m.   **BREAK**

PANEL I: KEY ISSUES AND TRENDS TO CONSIDER IN PLANNING FOR THE FUTURE IDEAL STATE OF HOME HEALTH CARE

10:15 a.m.   **Introductions**
Barbara B. Citarella *(Moderator)*
RBC Limited

10:20 a.m.   **Series of Presentations**

Trends in Population Health
Tricia Neuman, Kaiser Family Foundation

Trends in Public Policy
Douglas Holtz-Eakin, American Action Forum

Trends in the "Real World"
Barbara A. McCann, Interim HealthCare

11:20 a.m.   **Discussion with Speakers and Audience**

KEYNOTE: HOME HEALTH CARE 2024—THE IDEAL STATE

11:45 a.m.   Steven Landers
VNA Health Group

12:10 p.m.   **LUNCH**

PANEL II: WHAT WILL IT TAKE TO GET TO THE IDEAL STATE?: WORKFORCE

1:10 p.m.   **Introductions**
Margherita C. Labson *(Moderator)*
The Joint Commission

1:15 p.m.   **Series of Presentations**

The Value of Team-Based Care
Thomas E. Edes, U.S. Department of Veterans Affairs

Supporting Families
Gail Hunt, National Alliance for Caregiving

Direct-Care Workers
Robyn I. Stone, LeadingAge

Care Coordination and the Consumer Voice
Henry Claypool, The American Association of People
with Disabilities

2:15 p.m.   **Discussion with Speakers and Audience**

2:40 p.m.   **BREAK**

PANEL III: WHAT WILL IT TAKE TO GET TO THE IDEAL STATE?: NEW MODELS OF CARE AND APPROACHES TO PAYMENT

3:00 p.m.   **Introductions**
Teresa L. Lee *(Moderator)*
Alliance for Home Health Quality and Innovation

3:05 p.m.   **Overview of the Range of Models and Approaches to
                 Payment**
                 Peter Boling
                 Virginia Commonwealth University

3:25 p.m.   **Discussion with Speakers and Audience**

3:35 p.m.   **Specific Examples**
                 Jeff Burnich, Sutter Health
                 Richard Lopez, Atrius Health
                 Rose Madden-Baer, Visiting Nurse Service of
                 New York
                 Eric Rackow, Humana At Home
                 Ronald J. Shumacher, Optum Complex Population
                 Management

4:35 p.m.   **Discussion with Speakers and Audience**

5:00 p.m.   **Adjourn Day 1**

                 DAY TWO: October 1, 2014

8:45 a.m.   **Overview of Day**
                 Bruce Leff, *Workshop Co-Chair*
                 Johns Hopkins University School of Medicine

                 Elizabeth Madigan, *Workshop Co-Chair*
                 Case Western Reserve University

                 REFLECTIONS ON DAY ONE

8:50 a.m.   **Reflections by Day One Panel Moderators**
                 Barbara B. Citarella, RBC Limited[1]
                 Margherita C. Labson, The Joint Commission
                 Teresa L. Lee, Alliance for Home Health Quality and
                 Innovation

                 CONSUMER PERSPECTIVE

9:05 a.m.   Karen Marshall
                 Kadamba Tree Foundation

---

[1] Due to unforeseen circumstances, Barbara Citarella was unable to join this panel.

KEYNOTE: TOWARD PERSONAL HEALTH: GOING HOME AND BEYOND

9:15 a.m.   Eric Dishman
               Intel

10:30 a.m.   **BREAK**

PANEL IV: WHAT WILL IT TAKE TO GET TO THE IDEAL STATE?: INNOVATION IN TECHNOLOGY

10:45 a.m.   **Introductions**
               Thomas E. Edes *(Moderator)*
               U.S. Department of Veterans Affairs

10:50 a.m.   **Series of Presentations**

               The Evidence Base for Home Health Technologies
               George Demiris, University of Washington

               Telehealth
               Raj Kaushal, Almost Family, Inc.

               *Recommendations from the Trans-National Institutes
               of Health (NIH)/Interagency Workshop on the Use and
               Development of Assistive Technology for the Aging
               Population and People with Chronic Disabilities*
               Wendy J. Nilsen, National Institutes of Health

11:35 a.m.   **Discussion with Speakers and Audience**

12:00 p.m.   **LUNCH**

PANEL V: LINKING HOME HEALTH CARE TO THE LARGER ECOSYSTEM

1:00 p.m.   **Introductions**
               Anne Montgomery *(Moderator)*
               Altarum Institute

1:05 p.m.   Series of Presentations

               Connecting to the Larger Health Care Ecosystem
               Barbara Gage, The Brookings Institution

               Connecting to the Community[2]
               Joanne Lynn, Altarum Institute

               Connecting Data
               Terrence O'Malley, Massachusetts General Hospital

1:50 p.m.   Discussion with Speakers and Audience

                              REACTORS PANEL

2:15 p.m.   Introductions
               Bruce Leff, *Workshop Co-Chair*
               Johns Hopkins University School of Medicine

               Elizabeth Madigan, *Workshop Co-Chair*
               Case Western Reserve University

               Questions
               What does the future look like?
               What are the key needs and issues?
               How do we communicate the value of home health care?

               Reactors
               Kathryn H. Bowles, Visiting Nurse Service of New York
                   and University of Pennsylvania School of Nursing
               Judith Stein, Center for Medicare Advocacy
               George Taler, MedStar Washington Hospital Center and
                   Georgetown University School of Medicine

3:15 p.m.   Adjourn

---

[2] Due to unforeseen circumstances, Joanne Lynn was unable to make this presentation, which was given by Anne Montgomery of the Altarum Institute and Kyle Allen of Riverside Health Systems.

B

Speaker and Moderator
Biographical Sketches

Kyle Allen, D.O., AGSF, is the vice president for clinical integration and medical director of geriatric medicine and lifelong health at Riverside Health System in Newport News, Virginia. He is the former chief of the division of geriatric medicine and medical director of Summa Health System's Institute for Senior's and Post-Acute Care, Akron, Ohio. Under Dr. Allen's leadership, Summa Health System achieved national attention for research, innovative models of care, and success in demonstrating the value proposition of geriatric and palliative care to hospitals and the community. In his new role at Riverside Health System he is continuing this work to evolve a health systems approach to improving care for older adults and those with serious and advanced illness. Dr. Allen graduated from the Ohio University College of Osteopathic Medicine and completed a fellowship in geriatric medicine at the University of Cincinnati. He is board certified by the American Board of Family Medicine with a Certificate of Added Qualifications in Geriatric Medicine and is a fellow of the American Geriatrics Society. Dr. Allen is a researcher, book author, and inventor, has numerous peer review publications, and speaks to national audiences on health care and geriatric medicine. He is clinical professor of kinesiology and health sciences at the College of William & Mary, Williamsburg, Virginia. Dr. Allen recently completed the Practice Change Fellows Program (PCF) (www.practicechangefellows.org), a national leadership development program for geriatric leaders and clinicians sponsored by Atlantic Philanthropies and the John A. Hartford Foundation. He currently serves as a senior advisor for the Practice Change Leaders Project (http://www.changeleaders.org), phase two of the PCF project.

Peter Boling, M.D., is a professor of geriatric medicine at the Virginia Commonwealth University (VCU) Medical Center and an internist in Richmond, Virginia, and is affiliated with the VCU Health System. He received a medical degree from University of Rochester School of Medicine and Dentistry and has been in practice for 33 years. He specializes in internal medicine.

Kathryn H. Bowles, Ph.D., M.S.N., holds a B.S.N. from Edinboro University of Pennsylvania, an M.S.N. from Villanova University, and a Ph.D. from the University of Pennsylvania. Her program of research examines decision making supported by information technology to improve care for older adults. Her ongoing study, funded by the National Institute of Nursing Research, focuses on the development of decision support to determine the best site of care for those needing post-acute care. Other research areas include telehealth technology, home care, and evaluation of electronic health records. Dr. Bowles has been recognized for her research achievements. She received the Distinguished Alumni Award in Natural Science from Edinboro University of Pennsylvania and the Leadership in Nursing Research Medallion from the Villanova University School of Nursing Alumni Society. Her work has been continuously funded by federal and foundation sources for 20 years. She has more than 200 publications and presentations, she has served on the National Quality Forum Care Coordination Steering Committee and the Centers for Medicare & Medicaid Services Technical Expert Panel on the development of the Continuity Assessment Record and Evaluation tool, and she was a member of the Health Information Technology Standards Panel Care Coordination Committee to identify standards for the electronic health record. She was an invited expert consultant on transitional care, gerontology, information science, and telehealth for the Ministry of Health in Singapore. She is a fellow of the American Academy of Nursing and the American College of Medical Informatics and a member of the American Nurses Association and the Sigma Theta Tau International Honor Society.

Jeffrey Burnich, M.D., senior vice president and executive officer of the Sutter Medical Network (SMN), leads a network of nearly 5,000 primary care and specialty physicians that strives to provide consistently superb care to patients across Sutter Health in Northern California. Dr. Burnich works with physician leaders in both medical foundations and independent practice associations to identify patients' and doctors' priorities. Under his leadership, participating physician organizations have collectively agreed upon SMN participation standards and made a commitment to reaching and exceeding standards around clinical quality, patient satisfaction, patient wait times, online services, and clinical variation reduction. In addition, he oversees the operations of Sutter Physician Services (SPS), which provides health care practice management and administrative services to locations in California and Utah. The SPS team provides revenue cycle management, managed care administration, and practice management solutions. The Patient Service Center in Murray, Utah, logs 2 million calls per year. Dr. Burnich serves on the boards of both the Integrated Healthcare Association and the California Association of Physician Groups. Prior to joining Sutter Health in 2008, Dr. Burnich served as chief medical officer and senior vice president of system care management for the Mount Carmel Health System in Columbus, Ohio. Dr. Burnich was in private practice as an internist for more than a decade before joining Mount Carmel. He holds a bachelor's degree in biology from the University of Cincinnati and is a graduate of the Ohio State University College of Medicine. Dr. Burnich is passionate about health care delivery around the patient and providing quality and affordable care when, where, and how patients want to receive it.

Barbara B. Citarella, R.N., B.S.N., M.S., CHCE, CHS-V, is the founder of the award-winning company RBC Limited, a health care and management company specializing in disaster preparedness. In addition to consulting in all areas of health care, RBC Limited has worked extensively with local, state, and federal government agencies and the private sector on business recovery planning, protection of personnel assets, infection prevention, infrastructure protection, planning for all hazards, and the Incident Command System. She was a certified instructor at the U.S. Department of Homeland Security's (DHS's) Center for Domestic Preparedness. Ms. Citarella was appointed to serve as cochair of the National Association for Home Care and Hospice's Hurricane Katrina Task Force. She was part of the DHS committee to rewrite the DHS/Federal Emergency Management Agency *Disaster Preparedness Guidelines for People with Special Needs*. She also served as the conference coordinator for The National Pandemic Flu Conference held in Washington, DC. Ms. Citarella has also served as an expert on home care and hospice as a member of a panel on the pandemic flu for the Centers for Disease Control and Prevention (CDC), the American Medical Association, and the Agency for Healthcare Research and Quality (AHRQ). She was a contributing member to the AHRQ document *Home Health Care and the Pandemic Flu*, released in 2008. She participated in the CDC Pandemic Workshop for Primary Practitioners and the workshop for Long-Term Care. She was a member of the Association of Practitioners in Infection Control's (APIC's) Emergency Disaster Planning Committee. During this tenure she was a contributing author to *Infection Prevention Implications of Managing Haitian 2010 Earthquake Patients in U.S. Hospitals* (February 2010), *Infection Prevention and Control for Shelters During Disasters* (APIC, 2007), *Reuse of Respiratory Protection in Prevention and Control of Epidemic and Pandemic Prone Acute Respiratory Diseases in Healthcare*

(2008), and *Extending the Use and/or Reusing Respiratory Protection in Healthcare Settings* (December 2009). Ms. Citarella is currently the Home Care Section chair for the APIC. Her presentation at the 2014 annual conference was titled Health Care Reform and Infection Control. She is currently working with four state health departments that have received grants for needlestick safety and is working to involve home health care and hospice providers across the country.

Henry Claypool, having sustained a spinal cord injury in a snow skiing accident in college, has been living with a disability for more than 30 years. This experience has fostered a deep personal commitment to ensuring that all Americans with disabilities are able to access the services and supports that they need to lead productive and fulfilling lives, and this has been the focus of his professional life. In the period of his life immediately following his injury, Mr. Claypool relied on Medicare, Medicaid, Social Security Disability Insurance, and Supplemental Security Insurance. Support from these programs enabled him to finish college and pursue a career of service to others. Over his career, Mr. Claypool's work has spanned from the provision of direct services at the community level to work on federal policy issues in his most recent role in public service as a senior adviser to the Secretary of Health and Human Services. While at the U.S. Department of Health and Human Services (HHS), Mr. Claypool was a principal architect of the administration's efforts to expand access to community living services, which culminated in the creation of the Administration for Community Living. Currently, he is executive vice president of the American Association of People with Disabilities. In these roles, he relies on his unique background of public service and personal experience to seek pragmatic policy solutions.

George Demiris, Ph.D., is the Alumni Endowed Professor in Nursing at the School of Nursing and Biomedical and Health Informatics at the School of Medicine, University of Washington. He is the director of the Biomedical and Health Informatics Graduate Program at the School of Medicine and the director of the Clinical Informatics and Patient Centered Technologies Program at the School of Nursing. He obtained a Ph.D. degree in health informatics from the University of Minnesota. His research interests include the design and evaluation of home-based technologies for older adults and patients with chronic conditions and disabilities, smart homes and ambient assisted living applications, and the use of telehealth in home care and hospice. He is a fellow of the American College of Medical Informatics and a fellow of the Gerontological Society of America (GSA). In the past he has served as the chair of the International Medical Informatics Association Working Group on Smart Homes and Ambient Assisted Living and the lead convener of the Technology and Aging Special Interest Group of GSA.

Eric Dishman is the Intel fellow and general manager of the Health and Life Sciences Group at Intel. He is responsible for driving Intel's cross-business strategy, research and development and product and policy initiatives for health and life science solutions. His organization focuses on growth opportunities for Intel in health information technology, genomics and personalized medicine, consumer wellness, and care coordination technologies in more than a dozen countries. Mr. Dishman founded Intel's first Health Research and Innovation Lab in 1999 and in 2005 was a founding member of Intel's Digital Health Group, which recently formed a joint venture with General Electric called Care Innovations. He is widely recognized as a global leader in health care innovation with specific expertise in home- and community-based technologies and services for chronic disease management and independent living. He is also known for pioneering innovation techniques that incorporate anthropology, ethnography, and other social science methods into the design and development of new technologies. An internationally renowned speaker, Mr. Dishman has delivered hundreds of prominent keynotes on health care reform and innovation around the globe, including the Consumer Electronics Show, TED, the White House Conference on Aging; and meetings of the World Health Organization. He has published dozens of articles on personal health technologies and co-authored many government reports on health information technologies and reform.

Thomas E. Edes, M.D., M.S., is executive director of geriatrics and extended care for the U.S. Department of Veterans Affairs (VA). He has national responsibility for operations and management of the VA's spectrum of services, providing care to U.S. veterans with complex, chronic disabling diseases. Care is provided in all settings: in the hospital, nursing home, clinic, community, and the veteran's home. The services include geriatric clinics, adult day health care, home-based primary care, purchased skilled home care, veteran-directed home care, homemaker/home health aide, respite care, dementia care, community residential care, medical foster homes, community nursing homes, the VA community living centers, state veterans homes, geriatric research education and clinical centers, and hospice and palliative care in all settings. Under his leadership since 2000, the number of veterans receiving home-based primary care has tripled, palliative care has become an established program in every VA medical center, and the Medical Foster Home has grown from a pilot program to a national program in 42 states and is growing. Through his longstanding interests in home-based primary care and analyses of its clinical effectiveness and economic advantages, he has been actively involved in the development of independence at home, a component of the Affordable Care Act that began as a Medicare Demonstration of Home-Based Primary Care in 2012, providing comprehensive, interdisciplinary, longitudinal care in the homes of persons with serious chronic, disabling disease. Prior to taking this position at the VA headquarters, he was chief of geriatrics and extended care at the Harry S Truman Memorial VA Medical Center and associate professor of medicine at the University of Missouri in Columbia. There he was instrumental in developing geriatric evaluation and management inpatient and outpatient programs, subacute care and hospice units, a geriatric fellowship program, and the Advanced Disease Planning initiative. He was medical director of the VA Nursing Home Care Unit and the Home-Based Primary Care program. Dr. Edes served as associate director of the 1995 White House Conference on Aging Office and served for the Secretary on the Policy Committee for the 2005 White House Conference on Aging. He was instrumental in the VA End of Life Care initiative and was a project manager for the Institute for Healthcare Improvement MediCaring collaborative on improving care for persons with advanced chronic disease. His research interests included clinical nutrition, cancer detection and prevention, enhancing outcomes in home care, end-of-life care, and improving care for persons with chronic disabling disease. Dr. Edes received an M.D. degree and an M.S. degree in nutrition from the University of Illinois in 1981. He holds board certification in internal medicine and in geriatric medicine and is a fellow of the American College of Physicians and the American College of Nutrition. In 2010, Dr. Edes was elected president of the American Academy of Home Care Physicians.

Barbara Gage, Ph.D., M.P.H., is a national expert in Medicare post-acute care policy issues, including bundled payments, episodes of care, and case-mix research. She has directed numerous studies analyzing the impact of Medicare post-acute care payment policy changes, including the congressionally mandated Medicare Post-Acute Care Payment Reform Demonstration and the Development and Testing of the Standardized Continuity Assessment Record and Evaluation (CARE) Item Set. Dr. Gage's research has included numerous studies of the relative use of post-acute care before and after the Balanced Budget Act; case-mix analysis of long-term care hospital, rehabilitation hospital, skilled nursing facility, home health care, and outpatient therapy patients; the relative use of inpatient and ambulatory rehabilitation services; bundled post-acute care payment demonstrations; and the development of items to monitor the impact of the Medicare payment systems on access to and quality of care. She earned a Ph.D. in health policy and administration from Pennsylvania State University and an M.P.A. in public administration from the University of Maine at Orono.

Douglas Holtz-Eakin, Ph.D., has a distinguished record as an academic, policy adviser, and strategist. Currently he is the president of the American

Action Forum and most recently was a commissioner on the congressionally chartered Financial Crisis Inquiry Commission. He was the sixth director of the nonpartisan Congressional Budget Office (CBO) from 2003 to 2005. Following his tenure at CBO, Dr. Holtz-Eakin was the director of the Maurice R. Greenberg Center for Geoeconomic Studies and the Paul A. Volcker Chair in International Economics at the Council on Foreign Relations. During 2007 and 2008 he was director of domestic and economic policy for the John McCain presidential campaign. Dr. Holtz-Eakin is codirector of the Partnership for the Future of Medicare and serves on the Board of the Tax Foundation and on the Research Advisory Board of the Center for Economic Development.

Gail Hunt is president and chief executive officer of the National Alliance for Caregiving (NAC), a nonprofit coalition dedicated to conducting research and developing national programs for family caregivers and the professionals who serve them. Prior to heading NAC, Ms. Hunt was president of her own aging services consulting firm for 14 years. She conducted corporate elder care research for the National Institute on Aging and the Social Security Administration, developed training for caregivers with the American Occupational Therapy Association, and designed a corporate elder care program for employee assistance programs with the Employee Assistance Professional Association. Prior to having her own firm, she was senior manager in charge of human services for the Washington, DC, office of KPMG Peat Marwick. Ms. Hunt attended Vassar College and graduated from Columbia University. Ms. Hunt has served on the Policy Committee for the 2005 White House Conference on Aging, as well as on the Advisory Panel on Medicare Education of the Centers for Medicare & Medicaid Services. She is also on the Board of Commissioners for the Center for Aging Services Technology and on the board of the Long-Term Quality Alliance. She co-chairs the National Quality Forum Measure Applications Partnership Person- and Family-Centered Care Task Force. Additionally, Ms. Hunt is on the Governing Board of the Patient-Centered Outcomes Research Institute.

Raj Kaushal, M.D., is chief clinical officer at Almost Family, where his responsibilities include oversight of the company's 240 home health clinical branches spread over 15 states. Dr. Kaushal's expertise is as a physician executive. He is an expert in post-acute care management and has a unique background in clinical and management leadership, developing companies built on solid fundamentals and clinical excellence models, resulting in best-in-class clinical and financial outcomes. He served as chief clinical officer for home health companies valued at $300 million to $500 million and was a participant on the Home Health Quality Improvement Committee for the Alliance for Home Health Quality and Innovation.

Margherita C. Labson, R.N., M.S., is executive director for the Home Care Program at The Joint Commission. In this role, she is responsible for coordinating the efforts of the Home Care Business Development team in identifying new markets, familiarizing organizations with the accreditation process, and participating in new product development and the strategic development and tactical operations of the Home Care Accreditation Program. Ms. Labson is a veteran health care professional who has specialized in the provision of home health care services since 1977 from both multi-operational and academic perspectives. She has extensive knowledge in the legal, regulatory, and accreditation requirements for the scope of home health care programs provided in the United States and Puerto Rico. She is an experienced lecturer and educator, a published author, and functionally fluent in Spanish. From 1995 until late 2007, Ms. Labson served as a home care surveyor for The Joint Commission. She has served as both faculty and preceptor for surveyor education. She was previously the Compliance Officer for AMS/CMS Corporations in Miami Lakes, Florida. In addition, Ms. Labson has headed her own consulting firm, held managerial positions at a variety of home care organizations, and taught at the University of Akron College of Nursing. Ms. Labson received a bachelor's degree in nursing from Duquesne University in Pittsburgh, Pennsylvania, and a master of science degree in health care administration from Nova Southeastern University in Davie, Florida. She is a certified professional in health care quality and a certified case manager and was among the first wave of the Green Belts certified by The Joint Commission in accordance with its enterprise-wide program of robust process improvement.

Steven Landers, M.D., is the president and chief executive officer of the Visiting Nurse Association (VNA) Health Group, Inc., the nation's second largest not-for-profit home health care organization. As a certified family doctor and geriatrician, Dr. Landers places a strong emphasis on house calls to the vulnerable elderly and has a specialized interest in geriatric medicine, home health, hospice, and palliative care. Dr. Landers is a graduate of the Case Western Reserve University School of Medicine and the Johns Hopkins University School of Hygiene and Public Health. He currently serves on the board of directors of the National Association of Home Care and Hospice and the American Academy of Home Care Physicians. He has authored several articles on the role of home care in national publications, including the *New England Journal of Medicine* and the *Journal of the American Medical Association*. In 2009, Dr. Landers was honored as the National Association of Home Care and Hospice Physician of the Year.

Before joining VNA Health Group, Dr. Landers served as the director of the Center for Home Care and Community Rehabilitation and director of Post-Acute Operations for the world-renowned Cleveland Clinic.

Teresa L. Lee, J.D., M.P.H., is the executive director of the Alliance for Home Health Quality and Innovation (the Alliance). She joined the Alliance in June 2011. As a graduate of Harvard University's School of Public Health and with formal training as an attorney, Ms. Lee is a recognized professional in the fields of Medicare reimbursement and health law and policy. She brings to the Alliance a thorough understanding of the critical intersection between health policy, health care reform, and the law. As executive director, Ms. Lee hopes to support skilled home health's critical and valuable role as the U.S. health care delivery system changes to improve both the quality and the efficiency of patient-centered care. Ms. Lee has a strong background in health care policy and association management experience. Prior to her work for the Alliance, Ms. Lee served as senior vice president at the Advanced Medical Technology Association (AdvaMed) in Washington, DC. Her career at AdvaMed included her tenure as vice president and associate vice president of Payment and Health Care Delivery Policy. Ms. Lee has also served as a senior counsel in the Office of the Inspector General at the U.S. Department of Health and Human Services. A lifelong resident of the Washington, DC, area, Ms. Lee earned an undergraduate degree from the University of California, Berkeley, a master of public health degree from the Harvard University School of Public Health, and a law degree from the George Washington University Law School.

Bruce Leff, M.D. (*Workshop Co-Chair*), is professor of medicine at the Johns Hopkins University School of Medicine. He holds joint appointments in the Department of Health Policy and Management at the Johns Hopkins Bloomberg School of Public Health and in the Department of Community and Public Health at the Johns Hopkins University School of Nursing. He is the director of the Center on Aging and Health Program in Geriatric Health Services Research and the codirector of the Elder House Call Program in the Division of Geriatric Medicine at the Johns Hopkins University School of Medicine. His principal areas of research relate to home care and the development, evaluation, and dissemination of novel models of care for older adults, including the Hospital at Home model of care (www.hospitalathome.org), guided care (www.guidedcare.org), geriatric service line models (www.med-ic.org), and medical house call practices. In addition, his research interests extend to issues related to multimorbidity, guideline development, and case-mix issues. He has served on multiple technical expert panels for the Centers for Medicare & Medicaid Services on issues related to geriatrics and home health care. Dr. Leff cares for patients in the acute, ambulatory, and home settings. He directs the medicine clerk-ship at the Johns Hopkins University School of Medicine and has received awards for his teaching and mentorship. He is a former American Political Science Association Health and Aging Policy Fellow. He is a member of the Board of Regents of the American College of Physicians, past president of the American Academy of Home Care Medicine, and an associate fellow of InterRAI.

Richard Lopez, M.D., a physician at Harvard Vanguard Medical Associates, was appointed chief medical officer of Atrius Health in January 2009. In this position, Dr. Lopez works collaboratively with the chief medical officers and chief executive officers of the six Atrius Health medical groups on a wide range of clinical and quality initiatives. Specifically, Dr. Lopez's focus includes clinical program and regional project development, clinical aspects of payer/hospital contracting, clinical informatics, medical management, and safety and quality, as well as collaborating to develop quality standards and the outcome reporting measures and clinical dashboards that support the medical groups in meeting those standards. A more than 25-year veteran of Harvard Vanguard, Dr. Lopez has made many significant contributions to the organization and is the recipient of Harvard Vanguard's Lifetime Achievement Award. He also received the Becker Healthcare Leadership Award in 2014. Dr. Lopez received a medical degree from the Boston University School of Medicine and completed his residency and internship at St. Elizabeth's Hospital. Dr. Lopez received a bachelor of arts degree from Boston University and is a clinical instructor at Harvard Medical School. As a board-certified internist, Dr. Lopez has practiced primary care internal medicine at Harvard Vanguard's Medford practice since 1982. Dr. Lopez serves on several committees, including the Massachusetts Medical Society Committee on Quality of Medical Practice and the Massachusetts Statewide Advisory Committee on Standard Quality Measure Sets.

Rose Madden-Baer, DNP, R.N., MHSA BC-PHCNS, is the senior vice president of population health management for the Visiting Nurse Service of New York (VNSNY). She has practiced as both a nurse and a nursing leader in a variety of home health, managed long-term care, and community-based settings for more than 30 years. Dr. Madden-Baer is board certified as a public health/community health clinical specialist. She received a doctorate of nursing practice from the Duke University School of Nursing in 2012 and holds certifications as a professional in health care quality, as a home care and hospice executive, as a certified outcome and assessment information set (OASIS) specialist, and as a population health care coordinator through a postgraduate program at Duke University. Dr. Madden-Baer's responsibilities include creation of clinical operations improvement strategies and development of new evidence-based programs, including the development, implementation, and evaluation of a behavioral health evidence-based program at VNSNY. Dr. Madden-Baer has developed and disseminated evidence-based models of care that have informed community-based service delivery. In ground-breaking work that was also part of her doctoral research in nursing practice, Dr. Madden-Baer used predictive analytics to develop VNSNY's behavioral health program directed at the needs of homebound Medicare beneficiaries. She continues to build new care models for VNSNY. She has implemented several population health models (including two bundle payment models of care) using population care coordinators trained by the Duke University School of Nursing. Dr. Madden-Baer worked with other VNSNY leaders to mobilize teams of nurses and other clinicians and home health aides in community surveillance and the provision of public and behavioral health services to residents in the aftermath of Superstorm Sandy. This team was honored as a 2013 *ADVANCE for Nurses'* Best Nursing Team in the Northeast. Additionally, the American Red Cross awarded VNSNY an 18-month grant for $1 million to continue health, wellness, and behavioral health services to victims of this natural disaster. Dr. Madden-Baer is recognized as an industry leader with active participation in the Visiting Nurse Associations of America (VNAA), the National Association for Home Care, and the Home Care Association of New York. Dr. Madden-Baer's research has gained nationwide acceptance, and her work has been disseminated through her participation in national coalitions, podium presentations, and publication in mainstream media (including *The Huffington Post*); in academic journals and textbooks, including the *Journal of Nursing Care Quality* (January 2013); and as an exemplar in the textbook *The Doctor of Nursing Practice Scholarly Project: A Framework for Success* (Jones & Bartlett Learning, 2013). Dr. Madden-Baer's innovative work has brought her many honors, including being a finalist in the innovation category of the 2012 *New York Times* Tribute to Nurses, and then more recently, in 2014, she was recognized with a Distinguished Alumna Award by the Duke University School of Nursing and also received the VNAA Innovative Leader of the Year Award.

Elizabeth Madigan, Ph.D., R.N., F.A.A.N. (*Workshop Co-Chair*), is associate professor of nursing at the Frances Payne Bolton School of Nursing at Case Western Reserve University in Cleveland, Ohio. She has been involved in home health care as a staff nurse, agency administrator, and researcher since 1981. Dr. Madigan has also worked with home health care internationally and with the World Health Organization and Pan American Health Organization. Dr. Madigan has demonstrated the ability to lead, inspire, and support others while moving nursing practice and science forward throughout her career. She has a deep commitment to service within the profession and constantly works to renew the profession of nursing through her work in home health care, her mentoring capabilities, and her international work, all of which have advanced the profession and inspired colleagues around the globe to strive for excellence and improve the quality of patient care.

Karen Marshall, J.D., has been a family caregiver for both parents and is currently the executive director of the Kadamba Tree Foundation. She has helped her parents face a variety of serious illnesses and aging issues. She has cared for them both in their home and as a working, long-distance caregiver. These experiences inspired Ms. Marshall to establish the Kadamba Tree Foundation, which offers education and support programs to family caregivers. In addition to developing and facilitating these programs, she also advises government and community organizations on conducting outreach to help family caregivers effectively care for their loved ones. She also volunteers as a support group facilitator and legal expert for a variety of nonprofit organizations, such as the Alzheimer's Association.

James Martinez is retired and lives in Northern California. In October 2011, Mr. Martinez's mother was diagnosed with pancreatic cancer. He subsequently rented out his home and moved into his parents' house to help care for them. After his mother passed away in February 2012, he stayed on to help care for his father, who suffered from several chronic conditions. His father passed away in May 2014. Mr. Martinez says his experience with home health care, including the Advanced Illness Management and hospice programs, were tremendously helpful to him in caring for his parents.

Barbara A. McCann is the chief industry officer of Interim HealthCare Inc., supporting agencies in accountable care organizations, demonstration projects with dually eligible beneficiaries, and other alternative delivery models. Ms. McCann joined Interim in January 1998 and served as the chief clinical officer, overseeing the company's corporate clinical operations team, which developed policies, procedures, and practice guidelines for the delivery of patient care as well as compliance with federal laws and regulations and professional standards of practice. She also directed the national chronic care and transition programs. Prior to joining Interim, Ms. McCann was the executive director of accreditation, plan performance, and clinical management alliances at the national Blue Cross Blue Shield Association in Chicago, Illinois, where she was responsible for systemwide strategies for managed care accreditation and health plan performance data. From 1990 to 1995, Ms. McCann was vice president of outcomes management and analytic services at Caremark, where she provided the database and analytic support to six divisions of the company in the United States and abroad. Ms. McCann was also the first director of hospice and home health accreditation at The Joint Commission on Accreditation of Healthcare Organizations. She serves on several boards, including the Community Health Accreditation Program (CHAP), and is a Phi Beta Kappa graduate of the University of California, Berkeley.

Anne Montgomery, M.S., is a senior policy analyst at the Altarum Institute's Center for Elder Care and Advanced Illness and a visiting scholar at the National Academy of Social Insurance. From 2007 to 2013, Ms. Montgomery served as senior policy advisor for the U.S. Senate Special Committee on Aging, where she was responsible for developing hearings and legislation to improve nursing homes and home- and community-based services in Medicaid and to address dually eligible beneficiaries, health care workforce issues, elder abuse, dementia care, and community and social support services for older adults. She has also served as a senior health policy associate with the Alliance for Health Reform in Washington, DC; a senior analyst in public health at the U.S. Government Accountability Office; and a legislative aide for the Ways and Means Subcommittee on Health in the U.S. House of Representatives. Based in London as an Atlantic fellow in public policy in 2001 and 2002, Ms. Montgomery undertook comparative policy analysis of the role of family caregivers in the development of long-term care in the United Kingdom and the United States. During the 1990s, she worked as a health and science journalist covering the National Institutes of Health and the U.S. Congress. A member of the National Academy of Social Insurance and Academy Health, Ms. Montgomery has an M.S. in journalism from Columbia University and a B.A. in English literature from the University of Virginia and has undertaken gerontology course work at Johns Hopkins University.

Tricia Neuman, Ph.D., M.S., is a senior vice president of the Henry J. Kaiser Family Foundation and is director of the Henry J. Kaiser Family Foundation's Program on Medicare Policy and Project on Medicare's Future. Dr. Neuman's work at the Foundation focuses on a broad range of issues pertaining to the Medicare program and the population that it serves. Dr. Neuman is widely regarded as a Medicare policy expert, with broad knowledge of issues associated with the health care coverage and financing for elderly and disabled Americans and the health care of those individuals. She has published numerous articles on topics related to health care coverage and financing for the Medicare population, and has been invited several times to present expert testimony before congressional committees and other key audiences. She has authored and co-authored several papers and reports related to Medicare proposals; recent examples include *Raising the Age of Medicare Eligibility: A Fresh Look Following*

Implementation of Health Reform, Transforming Medicare into a Premium Support System: Implications for Beneficiary Premiums, and *Policy Options to Sustain Medicare for the Future.* Dr. Neuman has appeared as an independent expert on NPR, the *NBC Nightly News,* the *CBS Evening News,* the *Today Show,* the *PBS NewsHour,* and programs on other major, national media outlets. Before joining the Foundation in 1995, Dr. Neuman served on the professional staff of the Ways and Means Subcommittee on Health in the U.S. House of Representatives and on the staff of the U.S. Senate Special Committee on Aging, working on health and long-term care issues. Dr. Neuman received a doctorate of science degree in health policy and management and a master of science degree in health finance and management from the Johns Hopkins School of Hygiene and Public Health in Baltimore, Maryland. She received a bachelor's degree from Wesleyan University in Middletown, Connecticut.

Wendy J. Nilsen, Ph.D., is a health scientist administrator at the Office of Behavioral and Social Sciences Research of the National Institutes of Health (NIH) and the program director for the Smart and Connected Health program at the National Science Foundation (NSF). Dr. Nilsen's scientific focus is on the science of human behavior and behavior change, including the use of technology to better understand and improve health, adherence, the mechanisms of behavior change, and behavioral interventions in patients with complex conditions in primary care. More specifically, her efforts in mobile and wireless health (mHealth) research include serving as the NIH lead for the NSF/NIH Smart and Connected Health announcement, convening meetings to address methodologies in mobile technology research, serving on numerous federal mHealth initiatives, and leading the NIH mHealth training institutes. Dr. Nilsen Wendy is also the chair of the Adherence Network, a trans-NIH effort to enhance and develop the science of adherence. She is also a member of the Science of Behavior Change, Health Economics, and HMO Collaboratory working groups. These projects are initiatives funded through the Common Fund that target behavioral and social sciences research to improve health across a wide range of domains. Dr. Nilsen also chairs the NIH Integrating Health Strategies work group, which supports the science of behavioral treatments for patients with multiple chronic conditions in primary care. At NSF, she leads the Smart Health program, which targets science at the intersection between computer science, engineering, medicine, and health, broadly defined.

Terrence O'Malley, M.D., is an internist and geriatrician with an active nursing home practice at the Massachusetts General Hospital, where he provides clinical care, supervises trainees, provides network oversight of post-acute care, and conducts research on improving transitions of care and the exchange of clinical information at transitions. Until 2014 he served as the medical director of Partners HealthCare at Home and the medical director for Non-Acute Care Services within the Partners HealthCare System and currently sits on the Partners network-level steering committees for palliative care, readmissions, and quality measurement and is co-chair of the Transitions of Care Committee. At the state and national levels, he is the co-principal investigator and evaluation lead on an Office of the National Coordinator for Health Information Technology (ONC)-funded research project (Improving Massachusetts Post Acute Care Transfers [IMPACT]), which measures the effect of the electronic exchange of essential clinical data at the time of care transitions and its impact on the utilization of health care services. He also co-chairs the Massachusetts Health Data Consortium Transitions and Care Coordination Information Technology Work Group and sits on the statewide Care Transitions Steering Committee. At the national level, he co-chairs the Long-Term and Post-Acute Care Work Group within the Standards and Interoperability Framework at ONC, and he is a lead on the Longitudinal Coordination of Care (LCC) Work Group and the LCC Pilot Work Group. These groups created the data sets required to exchange a plan for home health care between agencies and the certifying clinician and the components of a longitudinal care plan with exchange standards for use between all acute care and post-acute care providers. He is a member of the National Quality Forum Care Coordination Steering Committee for the Care Coordination Measure Endorsement Maintenance project and serves on the board of directors of the Long Term Quality Alliance.

Eric C. Rackow, M.D., is president of Humana At Home. As president of Humana Cares/SeniorBridge, Dr. Rackow is responsible for the Humana At Home chronic care management platform. Dr. Rackow is also a professor of medicine at the New York University School of Medicine. Prior to his current role, he was president and chief executive officer of SeniorBridge, where under his leadership the company tripled in size to 44 home health agencies and a nationwide network of more than 2,000 care managers. Dr. Rackow joined SeniorBridge following a career in academic medicine, where he saw firsthand the challenges that frail seniors face in their homes and the need to provide personalized, ongoing support to prevent unnecessary hospitalizations and emergency room visits. Dr. Rackow's previous hospital roles include past president of the New York University (NYU) Hospitals Center, where he was responsible for ensuring the quality of medical services and promoting continued excellence in patient care, medical education, and clinical research; chief medical officer at the NYU Hospitals Center; and chair of the Department of Medicine at St. Vincent's Hospital and Medical Center of New York. Dr. Rackow is an expert in critical care and health care delivery. After earning an M.D. at the State University of New York, Downstate Medical Center, he trained in internal medicine, served as chief resident in internal medicine, and completed a fellowship in cardiology at the Downstate Medical Center. Dr. Rackow is the author of 184 articles and 40 chapters on the care of patients with complex medical problems. He is currently on the Board of Trustees of the Weil Institute of Critical Care Medicine, which is dedicated to education and research in caring for patients with severe illness or injury. He also serves on the Board of Trustees of his alma mater, Franklin and Marshall College. Dr. Rackow is a fellow of the American College of Physicians, American College of Critical Care Medicine, American College of Cardiology, and American College of Chest Physicians. Recently, he received the distinguished award of Mastership of the American College of Physicians.

Robert J. Rosati, Ph.D., is currently at the Visiting Nurse Association (VNA) Health Group, where he is working on the development of a connected health institute. Prior to being at the VNA Health Group, Dr. Rosati held senior management positions at the Visiting Nurse Service of New York and CenterLight Healthcare. He has more than 20 years of experience in health care in various research, analytic, quality management, educational, and administrative roles. Dr. Rosati is currently on the faculty Hofstra University. He has published more than 40 health care–related articles and has made numerous presentations at national meetings. Dr. Rosati is also associate editor of the *Journal for Healthcare Quality*.

Ronald J. Shumacher, M.D., F.A.C.P., C.M.D., currently serves as chief medical officer for Optum Complex Population Management, one of the nation's largest care delivery and care coordination companies for chronically ill, medically complex, and post-acute care patients. Dr. Shumacher previously served as executive director and senior medical director for Evercare of the Mid-Atlantic and as medical director and vice president of clinical delivery for UnitedHealthcare Medicare and Retirement, where he was responsible for the business operations and clinical programs for Medicare Advantage Special Needs Plans for dually eligible, chronically ill, and institutionalized Medicare beneficiaries. Prior to his position within the UnitedHealth Group, Dr. Shumacher practiced internal medicine and geriatric medicine in Montgomery County, Maryland, and served as the medical director of the Trinity Senior Living Community in Burtonsville, Maryland. He has extensive experience as a clinician and medical director in post-acute care and long-term care. Dr. Shumacher is board certified in internal medicine and is a fellow of the American College of Physicians, and a member of the American College of Physician Executives and AMDA— The Society for Post-Acute and Long-Term Care Medicine. He is a certified medical director in long-term care. He received a B.A. from Stanford University and an M.D. from the George Washington University School of Medicine and Health Sciences and completed training in internal medicine at the Georgetown University Hospital in Washington, DC.

Judith Stein, J.D., founded the Center for Medicare Advocacy, Inc., in 1986, where she is currently the executive director. She has focused on the legal representation of older people since beginning her legal career in 1975. From 1977 to 1986, Ms. Stein was the codirector of legal assistance to Medicare patients, where she managed the first Medicare advocacy program in the country. She has extensive experience in developing and administering Medicare advocacy projects, representing Medicare beneficiaries, producing educational materials, teaching, and consulting. She has been lead counsel or cocounsel in numerous federal class action and individual cases challenging improper Medicare policies and denials, including, most recently, *Jimmo v. Sebelius*, which will dramatically improve coverage and access to care for people with long-term and chronic conditions. Ms. Stein graduated cum laude from Williams College in 1972 and received a law degree with honors from the Catholic University School of Law in 1975. She is the editor and co-author of books, articles, and other publications on Medicare and related issues, including the *Medicare Handbook* (14th edition, 2013, Aspen Publishers, Inc.), which is updated annually. Ms. Stein is a board member of the National Care Managers Association, past president and a fellow of the National Academy of Elder Law Attorneys; a past commissioner of the American Bar Association Commission on Law and Aging; an elected member of the National Academy of Social Insurance; and a recipient of the Health Care Financing Administration (now the Centers for Medicare & Medicaid Services) Beneficiary Services Certificate of Merit. She represented Senator Christopher Dodd as a delegate to the 2005 White House Conference on Aging, received the Connecticut Commission on Aging Age-Wise Advocate Award in 2007, and is a member of the Executive Committee of the Connecticut Elder Action Network. In 2013, Ms. Stein was appointed to the National Commission on Long Term Care by U.S. House of Representatives Leader Nancy Pelosi.

Robyn I. Stone, Ph.D., is senior vice president of research at LeadingAge, and executive director at the LeadingAge Center for Applied Research. She is a noted researcher and leading international authority on aging and long-term care policy and joined LeadingAge to establish and oversee the LeadingAge Center for Applied Research. Dr. Stone came to LeadingAge from the International Longevity Center–USA in New York, where she was executive director and chief operating officer. Previously, she worked for the Federal Agency for Health Care Policy and Research (now known as the Agency for Healthcare Research and Quality). Dr. Stone also served the White House as deputy assistant secretary for disability, aging, and long-term care policy and as acting assistant secretary for aging in the U.S. Department of Health and Human Services under the Clinton administration. She was a senior researcher at the National Center for Health Services as well as at Project Hope's Center for Health Affairs. Dr. Stone was on the staff of the 1989 Bipartisan Commission on Comprehensive Health Care and the 1993 Clinton administration's Task Force on Health Care Reform. Stone holds a doctorate in public health from the University of California, Berkeley.

Sarah L. Szanton, Ph.D., A.N.P., is associate professor and director of the Ph.D. Program at the Johns Hopkins University School of Nursing. A number of years ago, while making house calls as a nurse practitioner to homebound, low-income elderly patients in West Baltimore, Maryland, Dr. Szanton noticed that their environmental challenges were often as pressing as their health challenges. Since then she has developed a program of research at the Johns Hopkins University School of Nursing on the role of the environment and stressors in health disparities in older adults, particularly those trying to age in place or stay out of a nursing home. Through a Robert Wood Johnson Foundation–funded grant, a National Institutes of Health grant, and a cooperative agreement from the Innovations Office at the Centers for Medicare & Medicaid Services, she is examining whether a program that combines home maintenance services with nursing and occupational therapy can improve mobility, reduce stress hormone levels, and decrease health care costs. She is also conducting a study of the Nintendo Wii program with frail older adults to see whether it can decrease their risk of falling. As a former health policy advocate, Dr. Szanton hopes that the outcomes of her research and her growing body of publications in the literature can have a positive impact on future health policy affecting older adults.

George Taler, M.D., graduated from the University of Maryland School of Medicine in 1975 and completed a residency in family medicine in 1978 and a geriatric fellowship at the Jewish Institute for Geriatric Care (now the Parker Geriatric Institute) in New Hyde Park, New York. Dr. Taler joined the faculty in family medicine at the University of Maryland School of Medicine, where he was an associate professor until he left in 1999 to join the faculty in the Department of Medicine at the Washington Hospital Center as director of long-term care. He currently holds the rank of professor of clinical medicine, geriatrics, and long-term care at the Georgetown University School of Medicine. His responsibilities include being codirector of the Medical House Call Program, vice president for medical affairs of MedStar Home Health–Visiting Nurse Association and MedStar Home Infusion Services, and medical director of the Capitol Hill Nursing Center, a 114-bed skilled nursing facility in Washington, DC. Community leadership activities include being past president of the Maryland Gerontological Association, 1991 to 1992; founding president of the Maryland Geriatrics Society (the state affiliate of the American Geriatrics Society), 1993; president of the American Academy of Home Care Physicians (AAHCP), 1998 to 2000; and chair of the AACHP Public Policy Committee, 2000 to 2014, where his interests focused on the development and implementation of the Independence at Home program as part of the national health care reform initiative. Dr. Taler was a member of the Board of the National Pressure Ulcer Advisory Panel from 2002 to 2008. In 2012, he was appointed to be the alternate representative for the American Geriatrics Society to The Joint Commission's Professional Technical Advisory Committee for Home Care and in 2013 was a member of the American Geriatrics Society Public Policy Committee.